COLLECTOR'S GUIDE TO
Vintage Fashions
IDENTIFICATION AND VALUES

Kristina Harris

COLLECTOR BOOKS
A Division of Schroeder Publishing Co., Inc.

The current values in this book should be used only as a guide. They are not intended to set prices, which vary from one section of the country to another. Auction prices as well as dealer prices vary greatly and are affected by condition as well as demand. Neither the author nor the publisher assumes responsibility for any losses that might be incurred as a result of consulting this guide.

Searching For A Publisher?

We are always looking for knowledgeable people considered to be experts within their fields. If you feel that there is a real need for a book on your collectible subject and have a large comprehensive collection, contact Collector Books.

On the Cover:
Left: A lingerie dress from the turn of the century, accessorized with a reproduction hat and belt, and a parasol c. 1880 – 1900 (p. 37).
Center: A two-piece silk dress from the 1860s, worn with the metal hoops and petticoat that its original owner used (p. 45).
Right: A silk velvet evening gown from the 1930s (p. 134).

Cover Design: Beth Summers
Book Design: Sherry Kraus

Collector Books
P.O. Box 3009
Paducah, Kentucky 42002-3009

Contents

Part One — The Fashions

Part Two — The Collecting

Acknowledgments

I must first thank the three sisters who grace the cover of this book: Joslin Gordon, Darcie Jones, and Stephanie Jones (from left to right). Not only have they contributed time and their lovely smiles to this book, but they have enthusiastically modeled for three of my previous books. You know, ladies, the books wouldn't be the same without you!

I also wish to thank their mother, Sharon Jones, who has always been kind and enthusiastic, and who loaned equipment and her home as the setting of the cover photograph. For angling reflectors and moving furniture and potted plants (and on a holiday weekend, at that), thank you!

I'd also like to acknowledge again each person who contributed photographs or items to be photographed to this book; thanks is gratefully extended to:

Karen Augusta, mail order dealer from North Westminster, Vermont;

Photographer M. Eden Banik;

B.R. Creations in Mountain View, California;

Donna Burns, a dealer who offers some mail order services through her shop *Amazing Lace* in Chatham Massachusetts;

Linda Collins of *Old Friends* in Eugene, Oregon;

Pam Coghlan, the proprietor of *Odds & Ads* in Rutherford, New Jersey;

Janene Fawcett, who offers mail order service through her shop *Vintage Silhouettes* in Crockett, California;

Collector Pam Horn;

Rosetta Hurley, a dealer who offers mail order services through her shop *Persona Vintage Clothing* in Astoria, Oregon;

LaRee Johnson, owner of the fashion presentation business *Victoriana*, based in Astoria, Oregon;

Barbara and Allan King, private collectors from California, who allowed reprints of photos from their own *Fashions Thru The Years*;

Julie Lassiter and Terry Cheetham, private collectors from Washington;

Linda C. McMurray of *Lydia's Timeless Accessories* in Fort Wayne, Indiana;

Tanya Zimkus of the mail order source *Tatiana Victoriana* in Charlottesville, Virginia.

Foreword

by Heather Palmer

After decades of hovering between the worlds of fine art and folk art, clothing has only recently been accorded its place as a vital document of social history. It has long been acknowledged that fancy and costly clothing of the past was to be treasured because of its beauty, but only in the last quarter century have museums and collectors treated even the simplest garments with their due respect.

Every extant item of clothing is a valuable document from the past. On the most apparent level, each item gives us information about the "taste" of the past. Further analysis into the study of the material, its dye, quality, weight, and the garment's construction gives information about the technology available when the piece was created.

Signs of wear and construction also provide vital information about the build, infirmities, and habits of former owners of the garment. The construction and hem wear on one particular dress puzzled me for several hours before I concluded that the woman for whom the garment had been made in the mid-nineteenth century must have had one leg somewhat shorter than the other.

Stains from blood on the insides of dresses, nightgowns, petticoats, and pantaloons are mute reminders of the monthly difficulties endured by women before modern sanitary supplies were readily and cheaply available.

Some of the lace and embroidered embellishments on clothing from 1815 to 1920 speak of the sewing skills of ladies of leisure, while other examples serve as reminders of the home "sweat shop" labor of predominantly immigrant women and children living in tenements.

Nineteenth century men's slippers needlepointed by sweethearts and eighteenth century busks carved by men for their fiancées are love letters from the past.

Our history is contained in our clothing, if only we will look with a discerning and trained eye, and if the documents endure for us to study. Because of the "come lately" attention to clothing as social history documents, there is an urgent need to conserve what clothing remains and treat it advisedly. An item that is altered by modern hands becomes only a pretty bauble, lacking integrity and information. An item that has been poorly cared for or amateurishly conserved offers a weaker quality of information. There is only a finite number of items left to us from the past and it is imperative for the education of future generations that we act as good custodians while the items are in our possession.

Barring natural disasters and wars, many of our possessions, if properly cared for, will outlast us, just as other pieces outlasted their original owners. Some items seem obviously fragile: ceramics, common sense tells us, should be kept clean and not be dropped. It is the dubious fate of textiles, however, to look more durable than they are.

The scholarly yet interesting lectures and many publications of Kristina Harris have already garnered her a loyal audience. Now she has done an important service to both museums and private collectors by writing this informative and thought-provoking book. A study of her valuable advice can point both laymen and experts to a clearer path for understanding and caring for clothing collections. If more people become educated in their appreciation of past garments, there is a greater likelihood that future generations will have wearing apparel to study, learn from, and enjoy.

Heather Palmer, formerly a curator with the National Trust for Historic Preservation and historian of Blair House, the President's Guest House, currently teaches college and writes on eighteenth and nineteenth century women's history.

Back in the old days (only a few decades ago!), nobody could imagine why anyone wanted to buy old clothes; they might be good for the kids to play dress up in, most folks thought, but why would anyone actually collect them the way people collect old china or furniture?

I remember once picking up a vintage copy of a museum catalog featuring lovely black and white photos of Victorian dresses; it had been published in the 1920s, and on the title page someone had scribbled "I remember wearing the darned things! And I don't want to remember them!" A little further down the page was a note dated to the late 1940s: "Somehow they look so much more beautiful than I remember them being...." Thus has been the life of collectible clothes: once thought nothing more than "rags," now cherished.

Happily, the number of people who admire and cherish antique and vintage fashions is increasing. It's easy to understand why. Only a few months ago, I found myself anxiously looking forward to an antique show coming to a nearby town. When I finally got there, I found it difficult to focus on single objects at a time; there were so many wonderful, old things to see! And when I saw a burgundy velvet and ecru lace turn-of-the-century gown in mint condition — well, that's another story.

The point is that collecting antique and vintage fashions is one of my great passions — just as it is for many people around the globe. To question what draws us to historical garb is moot. I, for one, am much more inclined to love a garment not just because it is beautiful (indeed, some garments in my collection are not exactly what I'd call beautiful), but because they have history. They tell me, as no other historical artifact can, how my ancestors lived — what their lives were like, how they felt about themselves, where their place in society was.

For example, I remember not too long ago looking at a pair of mid-nineteenth century

drawers with a friend whose husband was standing nearby. He looked over at the drawers with passing interest, but did a double take when he realized they were open-crotched. His face turning red, he asked: "Were they originally like that?" Yes, indeed they were! But Victorian women would have literally died of embarrassment if they'd thought that today their open-crotched drawers would be considered raunchy! Indeed, the layers of petticoats, hoopskirts or bustles, skirt, bodice, corset, chemise, rows of hooks and eyes, and difficult fastenings worn in the nineteenth century were undoubtedly intended to prevent flings of passion...but you can also understand that nature's call required convenience despite all those layers.

Yet clothing appreciated as a telling historical artifact has had a long and difficult climb toward recognition — one that is still continuing in some respects. Collecting clothing was begun in earnest in the seventeenth century in countries with royal monarchies (like Sweden and Russia), where pieces of royal clothing — in all their pomp and splendor — were carefully preserved. England (now one of the top countries for collectible garb) didn't follow this example — but their major museum, The Victoria and Albert Museum in London, began to collect clothing in 1844, only five years after Victoria took the throne, and three years after she wed Prince Albert. At this time (and up until fairly recently), the idea behind such collections was not to document history — for clothing was still considered too frivolous to be of historical value — but rather to "gather a lesson" for artists and craftsmen, and to tout the clothing's artistic and decorative qualities. Though this idea of clothing as decorative art would linger for many decades to come, in 1870 the museum's first catalog of fashions confessed that one of the rewards of fashion collecting was that it gave "a peep at the private female life in ages gone by."

The first historic fashion club seems to

have originated in England in 1883, but it quickly dissolved. England did produce, however, perhaps the most significant figure in the study and collecting of historic clothing: Dr. C.W. Cunnington, who had been a physician, served during WWI, and, by the end of 1930, purchased his first "gorgeous-looking old silk dress." At first he thought he'd have it cut up and made into a cloak for his wife — but then wondered if it was something that should be kept intact as an antique. No books on historic dress being available at the time, he took the dress to the Victoria and Albert Museum. According to the doctor, "someone there very obligingly examined it and declared it to be undoubtedly 'Victorian'," but could give no more exact date. So, like a trained scientist, he solved the problem of dating the dress himself. By amassing a large collection of nineteenth century magazines, fashion plates, letters, and the like, he soon became the foremost expert on women's dress of the nineteenth and twentieth centuries. And it wasn't until museums began to take clothing seriously as an historic artifact that they started to follow the doctor's example.

Dr. Cunnington authored some 10 volumes, gave lectures, spoke on British television, and generally brought about a public awareness of clothing as collectibles and artifacts. (So much so, in fact, that by the time Hitler had annexed Austria in 1939, the doctor received a letter from a lady in Vienna who asked that the doctor write to her requesting "the two dresses which my wife had accidentally left behind on her recent visit to Vienna." As the doctor concluded, "I guessed that this piece of fiction was in order to prevent the dresses from falling into the hands of the Nazis, so I wrote as suggested and received two very interesting specimens of the 1870s. I never heard from the donor.")

By 1937, America had officially caught on and a Costume Institute devoted entirely to the preservation and study of historical garments was founded. In 1946, The Costume Institute became part of America's foremost museum, the Metropolitan Museum of Art in New York City (founded in 1870).

It took some time for the masses to accept clothing as a collectible within their grasp, but when the resurgence of interest in antiques in general came in the 1970s, clothing was not far behind. The Costume Society of America, based upon a sister society in England, was founded in 1975, and by the 1980s, a number of books had been published on the subject of fashion history. Today, the antique and vintage clothing scene is booming as never before; several major national sales devoted entirely to clothing are held in the United States, and the number of garments featured at general antiques sales is rapidly increasing as antique dealers become more familiar with what collectors are looking for. Museums all across the U.S. — both large and small — feature displays of historic clothing regularly. Vintage clothing stores can be found in any state in the union, and I personally have corresponded with antique and vintage clothing collectors from all around the globe, including places like Italy, Puerto Rico, Israel, Japan, and the Czech Republic.

It was Heather Palmer (a woman who, at the time, I knew only through her good reputation as a museum curator and expert on historical fashions) who wrote to me suggesting the idea behind this book. I wrote back flattered, but skeptical. Yet as time passed, and I received hundreds of letters asking for advice on everything from storing a collection to what value certain labels gave, I realized that a book was definitely needed that was a general — but thorough — guide to collecting antique and vintage clothing, answering the questions collectors asked me daily.

At least five years after Heather Palmer's suggestion — here's the book....

A Word About Values

All values listed come directly from mail order dealers across the United States. Mail order prices tend to be more stable and consistent than regional shops and shows, so prices in your area, due to local demands, may be higher or lower. In cities like Los Angeles and New York, for example, certain items — like 1960s evening gowns — may sell for much more than they would in Eugene, Oregon, or even Chicago, Illinois. Auction prices are not used to consider values for this book because they tend to run higher than prices realized from other sources.

All values listed assume the item is in excellent condition. Any amount of damage, whether a small moth hole, tear, or stain, must be taken into consideration when trying to value your own collection. A 1920s beaded dress that sells for $220 in excellent condition, would be worth as little as $25 or less if it has a conspicuous stain.

Bear in mind that no garment is just "in good condition for its age;" either it's in good condition or it is not. Eighteenth century dresses exist that are nearly mint, and 1960s dresses can be found at shops and shows in a very poor state. Here are some guidelines to help in the determination of condition:

Mint: Garments that are like new. *No deterioration* of any kind.

Excellent: Garments that are in nearly mint condition, but have a very small amount of tears or stains *that are inconspicuous.*

Very Good: Garments that have tears, stains, or deterioration in small numbers. Defects still are not immediately noticeable and do not detract from the overall appearance of the garment.

Good: Garments that have a number of tears, stains or other deterioration that *do* detract from the appearance of the garment.

Fair or Poor: Garments that have a large number of tears, stains, and/or deterioration or garments that have only one flaw, but one that is quite noticeable; may be incomplete. Little value as a collectible, but may be useful for study.

All values in this book assume the item is in very good to excellent condition.

Example of How to Value Garments

Dress on page 128, approximate values:
In near mint/excellent condition: $400.00+
In very good condition: $200.00 – $300.00
In good condition: $100.00 – 175.00
In fair condition: $10.00 – 15.00.

Part One

The Fashions

Chapter One
The Gilded Cage

"One of the highest entertainments in Turkey is having you go to their baths," Lady Mary Wortley Montague wrote for *Godey's Lady's Book* in the 1850s. "When I was first introduced to one, the lady of the house came to undress me — another high compliment they pay to strangers. After she slipped off my gown and saw my stays, she was very much struck by the sight of them and cried out to the ladies in the bath, 'Come hither, and see how cruelly the poor English ladies are used by their husbands. You need not boast, indeed, of the superior liberties allowed you when they lock you up thus in a box!'"

The corset. Passed down by generations of women who locked themselves up in cages of steel, Victorian ladies adopted the original "gilded cage" as a necessary part of life. Today, it seems amazing that women went about their daily lives — housekeeping, bearing children, even playing sports — barely able to bend over, their middles crushed. Did every Victorian woman cry, "Tighter!" to her maidservant as the infamous fictional heroine Scarlett O'Hara did? Did the Victorian lady accept the corset thoughtlessly, not drawing any correlation between her tightly-cinched, 17" waist and her fainting spells? Though Scarlett turned up her nose and pouted, "Pooh! I never fainted in my life!," the truth is "to lace or not to lace" was a major concern for the Victorian woman.

"What a host of evils follows in the steps of tight-lacing," Victorian author Mrs. Merrifield wrote, "indigestion, hysteria, spinal curvature, liver complaints, disease of the heart, cancer, early death!" Is it any wonder women

took pause when considering whether or not they should corset themselves? Yet, as an 1888 issue of *Dress* reveals, a woman also had to concern herself with what might happen if she neglected her corset: "We have just received a letter," the editor wrote, "in which the writer declares that a woman's waist, left to itself, will grow larger and larger every year until it measures nearly or quite as much as the bust!"

The Thoroughly "Modern" Corset
The tradition of the corset was long and difficult to break (even ancient mythology spoke of Venus lending Juno her "cincture" so that she could entice Jupiter, her wandering, rake of a husband, back home); nineteenth century ladies felt fortunate that the corset had evolved into a considerably "modernized" contraption. *Peterson's Magazine* highlighted this issue in 1864: "The long, ungainly corset, as unbending as a coat of armor, and filled with whalebone and steel, oppressing the chest and keeping the body in close and painful imprisonment, has now been discarded, much to the benefit of the health and comfort of ladies...No French lady would think of wearing the old instrument of torture, as it is now called."

Yes, the new corset was a far cry from the old steel cage used not only to whittle down the waist, but to flatten the entire upper body. Nonetheless, even the less daunting Victorian corset had a marked effect on women's everyday lives. Not only were corsets required while "in society," but no respectable woman would (quite literally!) be caught dead without one tirelessly containing her torso. Rust-proof corsets designed for swimming, short corsets made specifically for horseback riding, corsets with elastic inserts for housekeeping, "electric" corsets that replaced whalebone with magnetic strips and claimed to "ward off and cure diseases"… manufacturers created a corset for every occasion.

Corsets even dictated just how a lady dressed herself. Her morning regime began by slipping on her stockings and (if her corset did not have attached garters) separate elastic garters along with them. Next, she would most likely put on her shoes, since it would be extremely difficult to bend over once her corset was on. Next came her drawers, and then her chemise — worn to protect her corset from body oils that would quickly make it necessary to have the corset cleaned by a special laundry-woman. Hopefully, the lady had a maidservant (or at least a sister) to help her into her corset, but if she didn't, it would take about a quarter of an hour for her to lace herself up. She would, as one writer described in 1837, "pull hard for some minutes, next pausing to breathe, then resume the task with might till after perhaps a third effort, she at last succeeds and sits down covered with perspiration." An 1871 issue of *The Metropolitan* described an alternative method used by ladies when "the size of the waist was of more importance than the size of the brain" — a mere decade or so earlier. "Fortunately," the editors chided, "there were bed-posts in those days, and any young lady who hadn't fortune sufficient to maintain a strong dressing maid took a little friendly assistance from those posts by looping her corset-laces about one of them, and then pulled her body away with all its weight."

Once this time-consuming process was complete, the lady was still less than half dressed. A corset cover (necessary to help hide the corset's bones once the lady was fully dressed), a bustle or crinoline, several layers of petticoats, and then finally a dress, still had to be put on — the corset ensuring that it all perfectly fit the figure, every time.

Dress described on page 147.

All-Important Corseting

Mothers (ever mindful of the fact that their sex was still denied the right to take care of themselves, and realizing that the more beautiful their daughters, the more likely they were to find "well-off" husbands) eagerly trained their daughters for the corset. As one Victorian mother put it, while she could not change the color of her daughter's hair, her height, or her facial features, she could very easily make her daughter's waist the fashionable ideal. Young girls of six or seven were often fitted with "training corsets;" though not heavily boned like the adult version, they were made from stiff cloth that fit snugly from the waist up to the armpits with wide shoulder straps to keep the girl from stooping her shoulders even slightly.

By the age of fourteen, very strict mothers graduated their daughters to full-fledged corsets — but even with the early use of a training corset, the transition was far from easy. "My daughter wore (the stays) the first night after much protestation, but on the second I found she had taken them off after I had retired to rest," one mother divulged, recounting the trials and tribulations of trying to give her daughter a properly whittled waist. "I then took the precaution of fastening the lace in a knot at the top of the lace-holes, and for a night or two this had the desired effect; but she was not long before she cut the staylace. I have punished her somewhat severely for her disobedience, but she declares she will bear any punishment rather than submit to the discipline of the corset." Her submission finally came, the mother declared triumphantly, after a month of corseting brought her daughter compliments at a party. "(Now) her only objection is that the corsets are uncomfortable, and prevent her from romping about..." Which was entirely the point.

Gown described on page 44.

Although such accounts seem cruel to us today, Victorian society insisted that a mother who loved her daughter corseted her. "I think history confirms that tight-lacing has a moral as well as a physical effect...The Puritan young ladies 'did not think themselves fine enough unless they could span their waists,'" one reader of *The Englishwoman's Domestic Magazine* opined. And, he further pointed out, in the few eras when the corset-less figure was in vogue and the term "straight-laced" took on negative connotations, there seemed to be a decline in morals.

A small-waisted woman was also considered more beautiful — and more marriageable — than a naturally-waisted one. "There is something to me extraordinarily fascinating in the thought that a young girl has for many years been subjected to the strictest discipline of the corset," another male reader wrote. "If she has suffered, as I have no doubt she has...it must be quite made up to her by the admiration her figure excites." Yet not all men found "charm" in wasp-waisted figures. "I believe that this supreme folly is perpetrated by women solely for the admiration of one another," another gentleman wrote. "I never yet met with a man who admired a small waist. Personally, I cannot conceive (a figure to be) elegant which approximates that of the wasp, an insect I could never yet bring myself to think handsome."

Corset Confusion

At the same time some doctors were claiming they could "scientifically" prove that without corsets women could not stand upright and would be as hunched-over as Darwin's early man, corsets were drastically hindering scientific knowledge about women's bodies. For much of the nineteenth century, for example, doctors believed that women actually breathed differently than men — their breathing not being abdominal, but thoracic. Little did they realize this was because tightly-laced corset prevented a woman's abdomen and rib cage from expanding. Victorian doctors also claimed that tight-lacing displaced "vital female organs," making the uterus sag — but it is most likely that such conditions were caused by frequent childbearing. Though doctors tried to bolster their claim that corsets rearranged the feminine body by pointing to the popularity of a rubber, cup-like device called the "pessary" (which manufacturers insisted held sagging uteruses more comfortably in place), the device was most widely used as birth control, before such implements were legal.

Is it possible that women were truly so thoughtless about their health? One popular myth has it that fashionable Victorian ladies had surgery to remove ribs — enabling them to obtain the tiniest of waists. Though it might be true that one or two wealthy women did go through the procedure, one only has to consider the extreme dangers inherent in nineteenth century surgery to realize this myth is far-fetched. The body still largely a mystery and germs still virtually unknown, survival rates after surgery were low; few women gambled on non-essential surgery when odds were so heavily against them.

Victorian fashion magazines are choked full of letters written by women bragging about their tightly corseted waistlines. Some ladies claimed to have 17", 16" — even 13" waistlines; yet an examination of women's Victorian dresses rarely uncovers an example with a waistline of less than 20". The writers of such letters no doubt took it for granted that the reader realized they were speaking of their corset size — not their waist measurement. When worn properly, the back edges of a corset do not meet, leaving a gap of at least 2" — and sometimes as much as 5". Therefore, a woman bragging of her 17" corset would have a corseted waist measuring about 21".

One young woman (who appropriately called herself "Common Sense") wrote to the editor of a fashion journal, claiming that even if a lady cinched her waist in 7" or so, she wasn't really crushing her middle. "Let anyone draw herself up to her full height by trying to touch some imaginary object far above her head," she wrote; "she will find her waist a good seven inches smaller...(therefore) the corset cannot be said to squeeze the waist."

Renouncing claims that corsets made women ill and could even be murderous, *The Metropolitan* speculated in 1871: "Statistics tell us that the number of women is much more than that of men, the world over. Now, the general use of the corset would very soon, we should imagine, affect this social distribution, were they productive of the fearful physical troubles supposed to be generated by them."

As a modern-day woman who has worn metal-boned corsets all day under Victorian reproductions and cinched in my waist some 5", I can tell you from personal experience that while tightly-laced corsets do make bending over difficult, they are not uncomfortable if they fit properly.

And so, while corsets were the Victorian lady's "indispensable," tight-lacing and tiny waists were far from being as prominent as traditional history would have us believe. Victorian corsets — though they may have been inconvenient — were something the Victorian lady felt obliged to put up with; as far as she was concerned, the advantages far outweighed the inconveniences. Not only did the corset democratize the availability of the beautifully fashionable figure, but, as one Victorian fashion magazine stressed, the corset gave "evidence of a well-disciplined mind and well-regulated feelings." Thus, the "gilded cage" brought the Victorian male down to his knees, while it safely held the Victorian lady respectably upright.

Dress described on page 37.

Buyer Beware
Today, corsets are prized by collectors. Easiest to find are corsets from the turn of the century forward, but earlier examples also exist. Too, while some corsets found today are well-worn, an amazing number are hardly worn or even in mint, never-worn condition. Some care should be taken, however, since corsets are currently going through a resurgence. Vogue, Cosmo, and any number of other fashion magazines have included layouts of modern "Victorian" corsets, and there are hundreds of places to buy these new corsets in the United States alone.

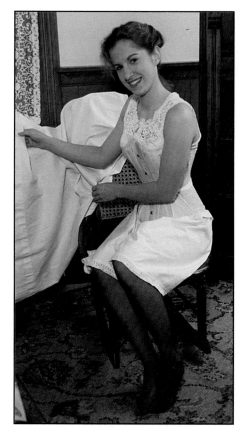

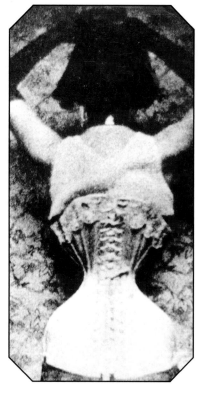

Most Victorian women never wore their corsets as tightly cinched as this woman of the early 1900s did.

A corset from 1837.

Nineteenth century undergarments. The corset dates to the early 1880s and has elasticized panels. The strings are new but are shown properly tied around the waist. The drawers, whose only decoration is a bit of lace at the hem, are open-crotched. Though a corset cover is worn under the corset for modesty, originally, it would have been worn over the corset; this corset cover features a crocheted yoke, and dates to the teens.
Corset, $150.00 – 200.00.
Drawers, $10.00 – 250.00.
Cover, $8.00 – 20.00.

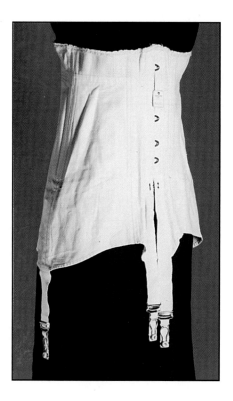

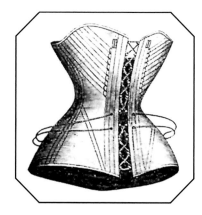

An 1850 illustration, showing how Victorian corsets were laced.

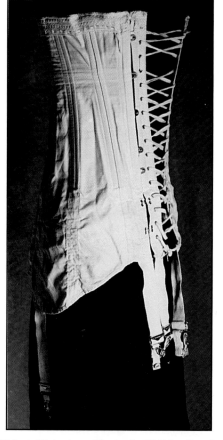

A "Parisian" corset from the teens.
$45.00 – 100.00.

Courtesy of Titiana Victoriana. Photos by M.Eden Banik.

Photo courtesy of Titiana Victoriana.

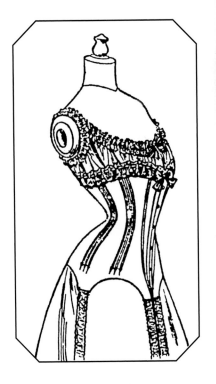

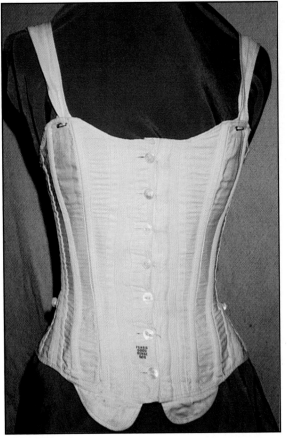

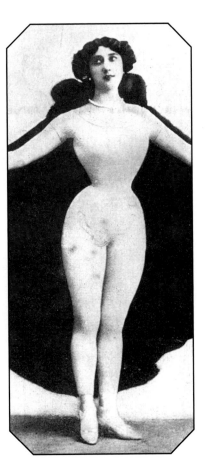

By 1908, when this corset was advertised, the S-bend look had taken hold, thrusting the bosom forward and the hips back.

A late Victorian corset. The buttons running down the front, along with the wide shoulder straps, indicate that it was either worn especially for sports, or worn every day by a woman interested in dress reform. $85.00 – 150.00

This photograph of a theatrical performer from the 1890s reveals just how breathtaking a wasp-waist could be if corsets were laced tightly.

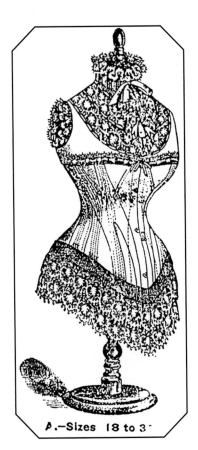

Striped and lavishly trimmed corsets were popular for special-occasion wear from the 1880s through early 1900s. The striped corset shown here dates to 1885, while the lace-trimmed one is from 1889.

A.—Sizes 18 to 3

14

Photo courtesy of Titiana Victoriana,

An early 1900s era corset. $30.00 – 75.00.

A corset from c.1850.

Courtesy of Titiana Victoriana. Photo courtesy of M. Eden Banik.

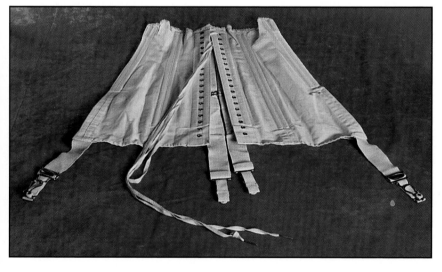

A corset from the late teens or early 1920; it is marked "College Girl, size 22." $45.00 – 75.00.

A corset shop's window display from the early 1900s.

Modern women have re-discovered the fun of corsets; custom-made to fit comfortably, corsets like this one of satin are enjoying a come-back.

Photo courtesy of Pam Horn.

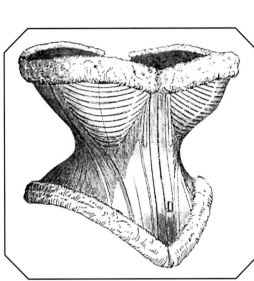

A fur trimmed corset from 1867.

This vividly striped corset dates to the 1880s – 1890s. $100.00 – 200.00.

This 1890s jacket-bodice is described on page 123.

Chapter Two
Chasing Hoops

The place is San Francisco; the time, the 1850s. A fashionable young lady strolls down the street with her tiny terrier, Poopsy. The dog is unlicensed, and soon lawful citizens notify the city's dog catchers about the rude little canine. When the catchers arrive, however, the terrier's brazen young mistress smiles coyly and lifts her crinoline just high enough for Poopsy to dodge beneath. The catchers take one look at each other and start back to their headquarters. They didn't dare...

Like Poopsy's clever mistress, some women found those cage-like, lampshade-imitating contraptions that held their skirts out in a bell-shape exceedingly helpful; others, however, found them to be embarrassing hindrances — sometimes even deadly. Though fashion-setter Empress Eugenie and her favorite couture Charles Frederick Worth are universally given credit for inventing crinolines, "hoops" were anything but new. First worn by ancient Cretans, hoops were revived periodically throughout history — most notably, in the Elizabethan era and the eighteenth century. And though Eugenie may have liked to take credit for the culmination of the hoopskirt, hoops were merely a natural progression from the layers upon layers of starched petticoats stiffened with horsehair crinoline that were worn at the time Queen Victoria took the throne.

Blame it on Eugenie

It all began when dressmakers added "slight whalebones" to skirts giving, as *The Ladies' Companion* described in 1853, "the ample fan-like form which is so graceful." Soon, women began contriving full petticoats held out with bands of flexible cane; this style became so universal that even peasant girls could be seen with canes in their skirts. By 1855, Empress Eugenie appeared before Queen Victoria and Prince Albert with her skirts held out by a "cage crinoline," or metal hoops. One of Queen Victoria's ladies-in-waiting reported that "the Queen was charmed to learn that Prince Albert admired Eugenie's toilette excessively."

By 1856, the cage crinoline was widely available to women of all classes. Quickly becoming a star in the manufacturing industry, women everywhere wore "cages" constantly (except when forced to abandon them while horseback riding, swimming, or sleeping). Even many nuns wore hoops under their habits; and actresses were notorious for insisting on wearing their hoops when performing historical plays. (One German actress, Christine Hebbel-Enghause, playing in a tragedy set in the Dark Ages, fell to the floor during her death scene, her feet toward the audience. As her hoops ballooned up, revealing her underthings, every man in the audience sat up a little straighter.)

Though Queen Victoria herself was often said to abhor hoops (the common verse quipping: "God save our gracious Queen,/Who won't wear crinoline"), she was frequently photographed wearing them. It is true, however, that in 1857 at the wedding of the Princess Royal to Prince Frederick William of Prussia, Queen Victoria forbade the wearing of crinolines. But not because she found them loathsome — merely because a crowd of hoopskirted ladies would never have fit into the Chapel Royal.

The Pitfalls...

The Queen was not the only one who had trouble managing women in hoopskirts. A taxi or carriage that once could carry four women comfortably, could now carry only two — uncomfortably. In New York, the omnibuses had such trouble cramming hoopskirted women onboard that they charged extra for any woman wearing a crinoline. Similarly, because the crinoline was among the first fashion articles to be available to all classes, factory girls and servants often got into tangles with their employers over the contraption. Not only was it considered improper for women of their station to own such a fashionable article, but cramped, poorly ventilated factories were further hampered by wide skirts, and maids knocked over countless shelves of bric-a-brac. One young Eastern girl who was hired as a servant by a Wyoming rancher and his family in 1867, reportedly grew tearful and angry when her employer's small kitchen could not accommodate her hoops. After a great deal of turmoil, the girl's employer drove a nail on a wall just outside the kitchen. As the girl entered the kitchen, she removed her hoops, hanging them on the wall. When she left the kitchen, she slipped the hoops back on. When, shortly after her arrival, the hoops disappeared, the girl cried bitterly, accusing her employer of destroying them. But the hoops reappeared that very night — on an Indian woman who wore them as she performed a dance in a nearby settlement.

The crinoline also had its dangers. Fatal falls down flights of stairs occasionally happened, and hoops were notorious for catching up in carriage wheels and steps, as one story in a June 1865 *New York Times* detailed: "A Young Lady Dragged Two Miles by Runaway Horses...as the deceased was being assisted from her carriage, the horses took a sudden fright and dashed off at furious speed. The young lady's crinoline became entangled in the steps of the carriage, and with her head and shoulders dragging upon the ground, the horses made the circuit of the village twice before citizens could stop them...."

Electricity still being a futuristic dream and candle, fireplace, and gas light being prevalent, fire was also a hazard to women in hoops. Lady Dorothy Neville wrote in her *Reminiscences* that the "monstrosity" called the crinoline nearly took her life. "I was showing a lady an engraving...which hung over the fireplace," she wrote. "Somehow or other my voluminous skirt caught fire and in an instant I was in a blaze, but I kept my presence of mind, and rolling myself in the hearth rug by some means or other, eventual-

ly put out the flames." Lady Neville was extremely fortunate, since it was nearly impossible to grab a woman caged by a crinoline and roll her in order to extinguish the fire. "None of the ladies present could of course come to assist me," Lady Neville explained, "for their enormous crinolines rendered them almost completely impotent to deal with fire." In December of 1863, at a Cathedral in Santiago, Chile, 2,000 women were less fortunate; they died in a fire begun on one lady's enormous skirts, then passed to the others. *The Illustrated News of the World* concluded: "Take what precautions we may against fire, so long as the hoop is worn, life is never safe. All are living under a sentence of death which may occur unexpectedly in the most appalling form."

Wind, too, could be a foe. Many women complained they could not walk down the street when the wind was up without being assaulted by lurid remarks. Western women, in particular, seem to have found the wind troublesome; when George Armstrong Custer was stationed at Fort Riley after the Civil War, his wife Elizabeth's skirts, caught in prairie winds, flipped straight over her head. Armstrong immediately cut lead strips for his wife and commanded her to sew them into the hem of her hoops and skirts.

Trying to be Modest

Because such accidents were not uncommon, another article of clothing became wide-spread: drawers. Open-crotched (often with each leg separate and held up only by a string tied around the waist), one young woman in 1820 reported that drawers were "the ugliest thing I ever saw; I will never put them on again. I dragged my dress in the dirt for fear someone would spy them. My finest dimity pair with real Swiss lace is quite useless to me for I lost one leg and did not deem it proper to pick it up, and so walked off leaving it in the street behind me...I saw that mean Mrs. Spring wearing it last week as a tucker..." Possibly having like experiences, many women avoided wearing the "ugly" and "masculine" garment. However, in Paris in 1855, one woman illustrated why drawers became important with often-clumsy hoopskirts. At a state reception, she tripped on her hoops and fell backwards, exposing herself to the Royals. King Victor Emmanuel promptly turned to the Empress and remarked: "I am delighted to see, Madame, that your ladies do not wear *les caleçons,* and that the gates of Paradise are always open."

Women soon began to realize that drawers were better than the revealing alternative, and by 1859 one of Queen Victoria's ladies-in-waiting reported that the Duchess of Manchester "caught a hoop of her cage in a stile and went regularly head over heels lightening on her feet with her cage and whole petticoat remaining above, above her head. They say there was never such a thing seen — and the other ladies hardly knew whether to be thankful or not that a part of her underclothing consisted of a pair of knickerbockers (the things Charlie shoots in) — which were revealed to the view of all the world in general and the Duc de Malakoff in particular."

Though the skirts worn over hoops could measure some 10 yards at hem, hoops themselves were never so wide. Skirts were meant to fall in large, graceful folds over the crinoline, which could measure as little as 60 inches around (or some 120 inches for formal occasions). Though they required a certain level of skill to maneuver when sitting and walking through narrow passages, hoops were nonetheless a definite improvement over layered petticoats, which invariably wrapped themselves around women's legs and made walking (let alone dancing) extremely difficult. "Many belles now wear 14 in evening dress," *The Ladies' Companion* complained in 1856. "They go to a ball standing up in their carriages, and stand between dances, for fear of crushing their dress and 14 petticoats!"

Men, too, had plenty to say about the metal contraption. Some complained the crinoline was a virtual moat, as playfully hinted at in an 1850s *Godey's Lady's Book* joke:

"George, you are looking very smiling. What had happened?

"The most delightful thing. I caught my Jenny by surprise this morning, in her wrapper, and without hoops; and I got the first kiss I've had since whalebone skirts came into fashion."

Other men seem to have found hoopskirts a romantic and appealing fashion; "Women are right to prefer these wide skirts, with their extravagant volume of material spreading over the ground," one man wrote to *De la Mode* in 1858. "...the whole effect is gracious...A young woman with a low-necked dress and bare arms, her skirts billowing out behind...could never appear more beautiful nor be better attired."

Men often found something playful about hoopskirts, too, and many jokes printed in newspapers during the 1850s - 1860s compared the hoops women wore beneath their dresses to the sort of hoops seen in play-yards:

"Frank, where have you been? You are in a perfect glow."

"I've been playing an old game — chasing a hoop in Chestnut Street."

In fact, the playful nature of hoops — reminding men of the toys they'd played with as children — might be the real reason the fashion emerged and lasted for so many years. That, and the occasional glimpse of ankle it offered.

100 Years Of Hoops

Perhaps because they are made of durable steel, metal hoops are still relatively easy for collectors to find today — but this hardly means they are commonplace or boring. It would be rare, in fact, for one collector to discover two hoops exactly alike; styles and shapes varied enormously, making hoops especially interesting for today's collectors. Especially unusual are cane hoops from the 1850s — and, from 100 years later — plastic hoops worn in the late 1940s and early 1950s (see Chapter 8 for more information on this phenomenon).

A one-piece silk plaid dress from c.1858 – 1863, supported by wire hoops. The buttons that run up the front are
covered in red silk, which is now nearly worn through.
The eyelet collar and cuffs were often referred to as
"broderie anglaise." Plaids were eminently popular during
this time period; the puckered look of this fabrics is testa-
ment to the clever and surprisingly modern methods of
fabric printing used even at this early date. $200.00 –
375.00.

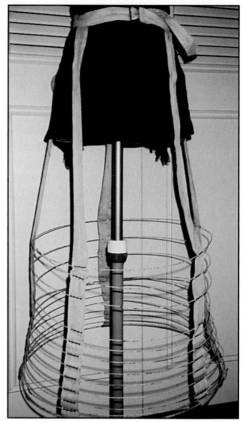

These hoops date to c.1858 – 1863 and consist of 30 rows of metal and five bands of fabric tape, closed with a buckle in back. The name of the original owner ("Whitehead") is written in pen on the waistband. $75.00 – 110.00.

These narrower hoops date to c.1860 – 1865, and were probably worn with a separate bustle. $65.00 – 100.00.

Notice how these hoops from c.1863 – 1869 are not perfectly round and flare out toward the back. $65.00 – 110.00.

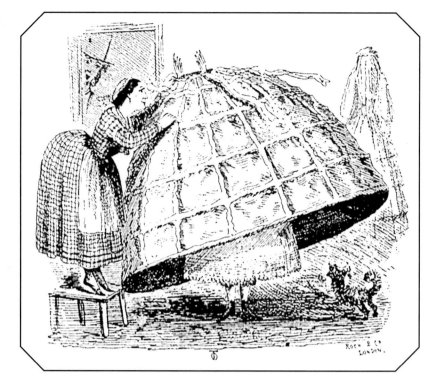

Caricatures often poked fun at women's hoops; this one dates to 1858.

A hoop skirt revival from 1921.

The classic dress of the 1950s: snug bodice and a full skirt supported by a crinoline petticoat or hoops.

Chapter Three
In All Modesty

Before Esther Williams made us all wish we were mermaids, before thonged bikinis, before (imagine it!) the *Sports Illustrated Swimsuit Edition,* swimming was a relatively mundane pastime. "Bathing," as it was then called, was little more than a way to cool off on a hot summer's day — men at one shoreline, women at another. But while modern fashion magazines may use the words "bathing suit" and "swimsuit" to describe the same scant garment, the truth is that the swimsuit is an entirely different species from the bathing suit. In fact, while bathing suits date back to the ancients, the term swimsuit didn't come into general use until the late 1920s. There's good reason for that.

Before the early 1800s, men and women generally swam in the nude. As the seashore began to take preference over pond holes, it became increasingly difficult for women to feel comfortable swimming nude — even if men were supposed to be a mile farther down the beach. For modesty, women began adopting "bathing dresses." These were as far from the modern bikini as imaginable: long-skirted and nightgown-like. Probably because many women's bathing dresses doubled as undergarments, most were utilitarian white, revealing, as one writer put it, "every inch of her womanhood" when wet. Soon, a less revealing shade of deep blue was widely adopted as the best color for bathing dresses, but the problem of modesty was still far from cured. No matter what color women chose, the hems of their bathing dresses always rose to the surface of the water. Naturally, weights were soon added to the hems of bathing dresses, but while this cured a modesty problem, it made drowning by entangled feet more common.

The Genesis of the Suit
Men, still preferring to bathe in the nude and avoid as much hassle as possible, didn't actually have a standard bathing suit until the 1850s when unisex beaches became more common. The Victorian man's bathing costume resembled strikingly his BVD's — disguised only by its bright color or bold stripes. As sleek and body-exposing as his bathing suit seemed, he wasn't about to change it for at least another 70 or 80 years. "Barefoot as a mendicant, your hair disheveled in the wind, the stripes on your clothes strongly suggestive of Sing Sing, your appearance a caricature of human kind, you wander up and down the beach a creature that the land is evidently trying to shake off and the sea is unwilling to take," one man commented in 1891.

As men moved onto their shoreline, women scrambled for something more modest and appealing to wear in the water. Nonetheless, both the unisex beaches and the suits that made them possible are quite remarkable; just consider for a moment what it must have been like for a young Victorian woman to glimpse a man on the beach. One bride wrote home to her mother in the 1880s in total shock upon discovering that her bridegroom wore night-shirts — so shocked was she, indeed, that she spent half her honeymoon "making him nice long night-gowns so that I shan't be able to see any of him." Imagine how she would have felt about his bathing suit! Too, imagine the Victorian woman's horror at being as "undressed" as bathing suits made her — not to mention the fact that she was forced to wear only a slightly feminized version of trousers, admitting to the world that she was, alas, a biped.

Still, by modern standards, the Victorian bathing suit — for either sex — was modest. Women now wore trousers or bloomers under a dress that reached down to the knees. "These," one ladies' fashion magazine commented in 1863, "are made in flannel of red, black with blue or red worsted braid; white is to be avoided for obvious reasons." (White may have been an obvious no-no to that fashion writer, but it certainly hadn't been to her grandmother — and even as late as the 1890s white bathing suits were sometimes worn. In *The Gentlewoman's Book of Sports*, author Mrs. Samudan wrote of a trip to Paris where she felt *trés chic* in her "ravishing 'get-up' of pure white serge...with...white silk stockings and sandals." However, upon diving into the water and then emerging, she discovered to her dismay that her "beautiful white bathing dress was quite transparent after such a wetting, and was evidently intended only for the 'Baineuses Parisiennes' who trip about on the soft sand and never let the water come above their knees.")

The new bathing dress was wool or heavy flannel and layered so that even when wet, a woman's figure was concealed. To add to their "neat appearance," bathing caps were worn, as were stockings and bathing slippers. The Victorian woman, caring more for her appearance than for her comfort while swimming, also wore her corset beneath. Though this was sometimes padded for a little more comfort, the padding made it weigh all the more when wet. Add this to the average bathing dress — which used six or more yards of wool and often contained weights in its hem — and it's a wonder women weren't drowning left and right.

"One of the chief reasons why males learn to swim easier than females is that they wear fewer and closer-fitting garments in the water — when they wear any," *Outing* magazine commented in 1888. "A woman's clothing interferes much with the free play of muscles, and when wet, constitutes a drag as the body is forced through the water." Their plea for reform fell on deaf ears, however, and eight years later, they were still touting their wisdom: "Our women must go through considerable trouble before they are ready for a dip, and to yet more trouble before they are again presentable after the bath. These facts are quite sufficient to keep many from the water, and in addition they have costumes to wear which effectively prevent the popularizing of the best possible swimming."

But the real reasons for the feminine Victorian bathing suit are obvious; women wore bathing caps to keep their wet hair from looking straggled. They wore corsets so as not to reveal their true figure to men on the beach. They wore slippers to protect their feet (a real lady never

went barefoot). And they wore stockings and a suit that covered them amply so that they wouldn't have to shave (which nobody did in those days).

By 1881, the feminine bathing suit could be sleeveless, and in 1886, one English magazine described and recommended a revolutionary costume: "Bathing costumes...of stockingnet in one piece with detachable short skirt (are now worn.)" The magazine did caution, however that "care should be taken less they reveal the figure when wet."

Nonetheless, the bathing suit was far from a standard costume. Children — unless they were from wealthy families — often ran about nude on public beaches, and many people sufficed with old clothes. "Some wear bloomers, buckled nattily about the waists, with cunning little blue-veined feet twinkling in the shallow water...others wrap themselves in crimson Turkish dressing gowns, and flounder through the water like long-legged flamingoes; some wear old pantaloons and worn out jackets," one newspaper man reported at the turn of the century.

By the 1890s a slight relaxation was found in many bathing suits. Corsets could be banished without fear of being thought "loose," and feminine bathing garb began requiring less and less fabric. "An American lady is surprised that English bathers do not wear black stockings as worn in the U.S.A. for mixed bathing," one English fashion magazine reported, adding the Americans' astonished remark: "You have no idea how decent they make the whole proceedings!" By the early 1900s, Americans were readily following the European example.

Indeed, as women's bathing suits became less and less, "feminine water sports" became more and more popular. *Outing* magazine frequently gave advice to gentlemen on how to assist ladies on the beach — even giving instructions on how to teach women to swim. "Make no promises," the editors advised in 1902. "Above all, never agree that a woman won't get her hair wet, for of such agreements come disappointment and distrust."

Such one-on-one teaching, which only naturally meant that men had to touch women's bodies without hesitation, shocked many people. In 1913, *The Ladies' Home Journal* ran an exposé on beach side familiarity with the blazing headline:

"How Much of This Do You Want Your Daughter To Share?" punctuated with obviously staged photographs of teenagers frolicking in bathing suits. "(These photographs) accurately indicate the free-and-easy familiarity that is continuous on these midsummer playgrounds from the opening of the season to its close," the editors warned. "Are these situations such as you would wish your daughter to share in, such as you would even care to have your daughter see? Where do you think such easy formality between the sexes leads?...Would you be willing for your daughter to take the chance of such familiarity, leading—"

The Inevitable Outcome

Despite the warnings of moralists, women had difficult choices to make. Should they cling to the old Victorian bathing suit — heavy enough to be called a "deathtrap" by some? Or should they toss aside their modesty and opt for a one-piece suit? The outcome was inevitable. "In an abrupt resolve to do the right thing," one middle-aged woman wrote in the teens, "I had donned a one-piece suit. I am not a large woman, not fat; that is, not as fat as many others whom I could name, but a one-piece suit stretched over one hundred and eighty-five fairish pounds, feels as conspicuous as a red letter. I know." The age when anyone without a perfect body could roam the beach self-assured was never again to be seen. The new feminine suit had a scooping neckline, short or non-existent sleeves, shorts ending just above the knee (or sometimes even at mid-thigh). The only modesty provided was a scant skirt that barely hid the end of the legs.

Though men's suits were also becoming briefer (bathing trunks were even introduced — though they were unsuitable for actual swimming since they weighed nine pounds when wet and had an annoying tendency of falling down), it was women's bathing attire that was in the limelight. So much so, in fact, that by 1916, Madison Square Garden held one of the first bathing suit contests. Of the winner — who wore a zebra-striped suit — a man from Ohio commented: "Well, it may be her own creation, but I know she didn't have to work overtime to create it. A spider could create as much in about three minutes."

No longer intended to cover modestly — rather the opposite, in fact — the swimsuit was born. Though *Vogue* would later comment that "it took a certain amount of courage for the bathing-girl to appear in this daring costume and she really deserves the credit for firing the first shot in the Battle of Modern Dress," the swimsuit really had more to do with a sexual revolution than a dress or feminist revolution. Where the Victorian woman had hid shyly behind the layers of wool that made up her bathing suit, women who first dared to wear the swimsuit were coquettishly flaunting nudity — not quite, but almost, revealed.

The Incredible Shrinking Suit

In 1930 *Men's Wear* made mention of the newest style of women's suits: "Manufacturers are selling women's bathing suits that are scantier than ever. Backs are open to the last vertebrae, armholes are wider, and altogether women's bathing suits...will be practically nothing to speak of." And forget wool and flannel, the latest bathing suits were constructed of new man-made materials, including "Lastex" and "Contralex" (which women loved because they helped to slim the figure). As early as 1935 the bikini appeared — though it was far from widely worn, as it left "some inches of flesh exposed between its two parts." Another innovation — though short-lived — was Jantzen's "wisp-o-weight." Made up in flesh tones, at first glance the bathing beauty who donned it gave the impression she was nude.

In the 1940s, sex appeal unquestionably became the true aim of women's bathing suits, and manufacturers took full advantage of this fact. Jantzen, for example, introduced the "Beauty-Life Bra" built into their suits, in addition to tummy and hip-flattening girdles and waist-nippers. Nonetheless, suits were generally less revealing, often featuring scant, ruffled skirts. Trimming became a part of women's swimwear for the first time since the early 1900s, and sweetheart necklines were supreme. By 1949, the strapless bathing suit was leading women into the 1950s — though it's doubtful most women were able to actually swim in them. The bikini, though still modest by modern standards, was slowly becoming more scant and was said to "reveal everything about a girl except her mother's maiden name."

Most bathing suits from the 1950s are immediately recognizable by their fabrics. Either the color tips you off (you know, bright pink, bright green and yellow, etc.), or the print simply reeks '50s (like a Hawaiian design). Another innovation of the late '40s and early '50s, however — the playsuit — can be a confusion. Playsuits were generally short-skirted contraptions worn over attached bloomers and often had a full blouse that could be worn with it. Some bathing suits of the period are very much the same. But generally only the bathing suits will have built-in foundations (including heavy bosom-padding and feather-boning).

By 1959, *The New York Times* ran a headline that pretty much sums up the late 1950s forward: "Bikini Is in the Swim of Things Again: Sudden Popularity Here Is a Mystery."

More than any other type of fashion, the bathing suit reveals the deepest secrets of our ancestors. Listen to *Vogue* in 1922: "Gone are the days when a bathing suit was simply a covering that would wring out well. Today, one's individuality must be considered..." and "Aphrodite rising from the foam may have been dazzlingly beautiful, but these three graces are convinced that foam as a decorative adjunct may be overdone..." Or in 1950: "The bathing suit has acquired a new state of — dress, not undress..." Or in 1970: "Bright little strips of bathing suits with new twists and ties, ready now to make you look marvelous..." And possibly the most astute, from the 1920s: "It took a certain amount of courage for the bathing-girl to appear in this daring (one-piece) costume, and she really deserved the credit for firing the first shot in the Battle of Modern Dress."

My, what Esther Williams would have said! "Why they come off in the water," she actually did exclaim in her own special naiveté. "If you can't swim in them, what good are they?"

Collecting Bathing Suits

Bathing suits are largely ignored in the world of collectible fashions — yet they are an intriguing addition to any costume collection. Though it's doubtful that any collector is likely to run across an early nightgown-like bathing dress, Victorian bathing suits are definitely available. Even easier to find are suits from the 1920s forward. I have yet to find any suit from before the early 1900s that has a label sewn into it, but by the 1920s, J.C. Penney labels are common, as are Jantzen labels and Jantzen's easy-to-recognize "Diving Girl" appliqué sewn onto the outside of the garment. Most suits from this time forward have some sort of label — which is nice because very often you can research ads that will help you pinpoint the date of the suit.

Quite often wool suits are in a sad state. If the moths haven't gotten to them, that old-wool and mothballs stench has. The latter is easily remedied by washing. Wool suits should be wrapped in an old cotton sheet and stored with an herbal moth repellent to ward off pests.

A 1940s starlet in a "glamorous" two-piece bikini.

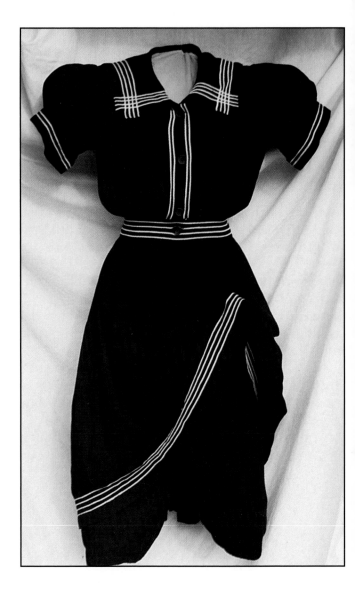

This wool crepe bathing suit from the mid-to late-1890s consists of two separate pieces: a bodice with attached bloomers, and a skirt that buttons on at the waist. Suits like these were considered quite contemporary and were less cumbersome and more practical than any bathing suit had ever been previously. $85.00 – 110.00.

This nineteenth century trade card for sewing thread illustrates the way many Victorians appeared at the beach: in full, everyday, impractical attire.

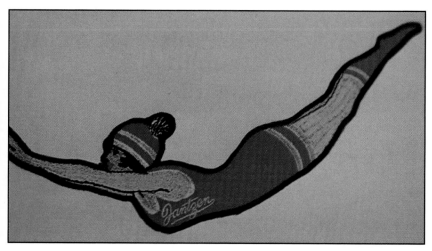

The Jantzen "Diving Girl" appeared on all Jantzen suits.

An early Jantzen ad.

Courtesy of Titiana Victoriana
Photo by M. Eden Banik.

Velvet suits with gathered or ruched accents were exceedingly popular in the mid to late 1940s. $65.00 – 95.00.

A flapper in a classic 1920s bathing suit of wool serge. Her rolled hose and bathing slippers are typical.

Chapter Four

On Black...

Most women love to wear black. And why shouldn't we? The moment somebody told us black made us look thinner, what else was to be expected?

Historical fashion collectors will also find black to be one of the most readily available types of collectible clothing. The best of both worlds? I think so. Yet black vintage clothing has developed a sort of stigma in the collecting world; it is said to be too readily available — and therefore not as valuable as other types of vintage clothes.

Well, humbug. I don't know who came up with this idea (probably a collector who wanted to hoard black vintage clothes — her favorites — for herself), but I think it is just plain silly.

First of all, aren't some of the most important fashion collections in museums made up of clothes "everyday, typical" people wore? After years of struggling to make the importance of "average" historical garments known, many museum curators would love to challenge anyone who claimed "typical" historical clothes were not valuable.

Black clothes tell us a great deal about our ancestors. Unlike modern women, most women before the turn of the century didn't wear black because they thought it made them look thinner; there were more fundamental reasons for the wearing of black.

Consider, for instance, the state of clothes cleaning before the automatic washer and dryer in the 1950s.

You've heard the old nursery rhyme: "This is the way we wash our clothes early Monday morning?" Our ancestors were probably fortunate if the washing didn't take until Thursday to finish. Washable clothes had to be separated, soaked, boiled, rinsed, blued, wrung out, starched, hung, and ironed — by hand. Unwashable clothes were thoroughly brushed down or rubbed with flour before being starched and ironed. And then there was the rest of the housework to do. As one turn-of-the-century housekeeping book put it: "Make all possible preparations the day before the washing. Do not bake and cook more than is necessary on washing day. Have two or three staple dishes prepared... for you will need all your strength for the hard day's work."

Black, therefore, was the most practical of all colors for clothes — particularly for clothing that could not be washed — because dirt and soil would not show up as easily. (Corsets were often made in black for this very reason.) It's a little unpleasant to think of our ancestors wearing never-washed clothes — but there were few alternatives before chemical dry cleaning.

Black clothes were practical for other reasons also. In days when the average woman owned about half (or less) the clothing today's average woman owns, clothes had to be wearable in a variety of places. A black silk dress, for example, could be "dressed down" for church, "dressed up" for a party, and perhaps even be worn for traveling. Black would also hide wear and tear better than most other colors; it hasn't been until recently that restyling and repairing clothes have gone out of fashion.

You will notice I haven't mentioned black for mourning, which is what most people assume black historical clothes were for. First of all, not everyone wore black for mourning, just as they don't today; some people even chose to wear white for mourning. Do you wear black only when you are in mourning? Victorians were no different.

It is true that Victorians, in particular, made a ritual out of mourning the dead. Queen Victoria (the lady that all ladies of the nineteenth century tried to emulate) mourned in black for Prince Albert for 40 years. Such cases were extreme, however; most Victorian women mourned in black for their husbands or children no longer than a year — less for other people. Still, with the mortality rate as high as it was in the nine-teenth century, I suppose it is possible a lady could be in mourning for a good deal of her life — possible, but unlikely.

There are, no doubt, a variety of other reasons black has been so popular and important in fashion history that I have failed to mention here — but do collectors need any more reasons to poo-poo the idea that black is quasi-collectible? If part of the collectability of clothes lies in the preserved history captured in them, then black is, contrarily, an important addition to every vintage clothing collection.

This black and white ensemble from the 1860s consists of a white tucked shirtwaist featuring eyelet and a black ribbon trim at the neck, a black bolero trimmed with lace, and a black grosgrain belt with a metal buckle.
Shirtwaist, $50.00 – $70.00. Bolero, $50.00 – 70.00. Belt, $20.00 – 25.00.

This bodice, dating to the early 1900s, is fashioned from robin's egg blue silk overlaid with black lace. $95.00 – 120.00.

Photo courtesy of the Lassiter/Cheetham collection.

A homemade black velvet dress from the 1920s, showcasing beaded flowers, an ecru lace collar, and a satin ribbon that is tacked to the neckline, and tucks through a slit in front. $50.00 – 95.00.

A c.1902 – 1906 two-piece silk dress. $85.00 – 165.00.

During the 1890s, many mantles and capelets were made entirely of jet beading. An illustration from an 1887 issue of *Ladies' Home Journal* reveals that this type of garment was called a "chemisette" in its day. $100.00 – 200.00.

A black bodice that may have been worn for mourning. The sleeves were originally much larger, in the c.1894 – 1896 style, but were later tacked down in a style more popular around 1897. $25.00 – 40.00.

Chapter Five
...And White

At the turning of the nineteenth century, Sears catalog featured laces and sheer embroideries more than any other type of fabric — and over half of their offered ready-made dresses were white. Certainly Sears was not alone in this phenomenon. Bloomingdale's also followed suit — as did every fashionable catalog, clothing shoppe, dressmaker, and designer. Even fashion plates featured these so-called "lingerie dresses" — which, true to their name, deftly impersonated undergarments. The floral whitework, romantic puffing and shirring, delicious lace insets, rich silk ribbons, and detailed pintucking had once been reserved solely for a lady's most private garments — but finally, it seemed, boudoir garments had pinnacled to such extravagance, they could no longer bear to be concealed.

But this was not a sudden phenomenon. Since Marie Antoinette first refused the fictitious, angular clothing of the early 1780s and adopted the more fluid, soft, boudoir-look of her *chemise a la reine*, the desire for whites became fashionable. At first thought shockingly brazen, the style quietly persisted until circa 1800, when most fashionable ladies wore the sheer, slender, Empire style that is so identified with the onset of the nineteenth century.

Though the white look faded away in the 1820s, making only rare appearances in evening wear, by the mid-1860s it was making a strong come-back. By this time, however, the look had taken on new meaning. Perhaps because the invention of the sewing machine made dressmakers' wildest fantasies more probable, the new look was far more flamboyant. Ruffles and frills abounded — and in traditional Victorian style if a few frills were thought good, then more were thought better. Flimsy "invisible" dresses of gauze, net, and fine silk were favored in white shades — always embellished with tucks, ruching, and lace.

Still, from the 1820s to the 1880s, whites were mostly reserved for the wealthy — for who but the wealthy could afford the impracticality of a white wardrobe? By the 1890s, however, the white dress phenomenon invaded all classes. In fact, the white dress filled what might otherwise have been an awkward void between an era when women freed themselves from the enormous weight of opulent dresses, and an era when women began to dress in a more tailored fashion.

The new availability of machine-made laces had a great deal to do with the "lingerie" look; where once every woman had dreamed of a beautifully flowing lace dress — but only the rich could indulge — now nearly every woman could add the new fairy-tale-like dress style to her wardrobe. In 1894 *The Ladies Home Journal* pointed out, "White gowns are usually counted on as expensive...they soil so easily and necessitate visits either to the laundry or the cleaners that cost so much...Yet with care, one may be worn an entire season."

On the other hand, some *fin de siécle* women were quick to condemn the new fashion. In her book *From A Girl's Point Of View*, author Lilian Bell complained: "...a word with you, you dear, unsophisticated man. I have heard you, with sound of your hundred-and-fifty-dollar-a-month salary ringing in your ears, gurgle and splash about a girl who wears 'simple white muslins' to balls; and I have heard you set down, as extravagant, and too rich for your purse, the girl who wears silk. There is no more extravagant or troublesome gown in the world than what you call a 'simple white muslin.' In the first place, it never is muslin, unless it is Paris muslin, which is no joke, if you are thinking of paying for it yourself, as it necessitates a silk lining, which costs more than the outside. If it's trimmed with lace, that would take as much of your salary as the coal for all winter would come to. If trimmed with ribbons, they must be changed often to freshen the gown, whose only beauty is its freshness...If it can be worn five times during the winter, the girl is either a careful dancer or else a wallflower. In either case, after every wearing she must have it pressed out and put away as daintily as if it were egg-shells, all of which is the greatest nuisance on earth. Often such a gown is torn all to pieces the first time it is worn. Scores of 'simple white muslin' ball-gowns at a hundred dollars apiece are only worn once or twice."

The Delineator had less condemning words for the lingerie dress and its soft white fabric. "More sheer than ever are the fabrics displayed for summer gowns..." the editors commented in 1902. "Veiling is the more approved material...Some of the choicest samples of this goods (sic.) are so fine and thin as to resemble the daintiest of mousselines...But despite all the charming tints (available) white is in highest favor and for all occasions...Indeed, the entire Summer outfit may be in white...White batiste is a dainty fabric and suggests fascinating toilettes when associated with the embroidered batiste or white all-over lace. These dresses are made unlined and are intended to be worn over colored silk foundations...The designs by which these dresses are developed are sufficiently simple to make it possible for the home-dressmaker easily to construct them." The idea of a sheer dress worn over colored slips, underdresses, or "guimpes" was especially popular among ladies with little funds for a new wardrobe.

The fragile materials used to make lingerie dresses have made them particularly vulnerable. Fortunately, however, such dresses are so exquisite that the original and subsequent owners have usually taken special care with them, and now they are very popular among collectors.

The fabrics used in the majority of white dresses found by collectors today are usually superior cottons and occasionally silks (the cottons often feel much like silk); these have been more durable then the batistes and chiffons sometimes used. Frequently, small holes or rips are discovered in the more affordable whites found by today's collector, but these can be quickly mended by hand without appearing conspicuous. More difficult is washing these lovely old dresses.

It is important to point out that many old whites aren't actually "white" in color; often they are off-white, or even a bluish-white. Therefore, no amount of washing will turn them into the pure white of most modern clothes. However, if you tend to buy your vintage clothes untouched by caring hands, no doubt your whites will be more brown than anything else, and a gentle washing will be necessary. For more information on washing, read pages 95 and 97.

Your whites will need to be treated tenderly, but they add a dash of romance to your collection that no other piece of clothing can!

A picturesque scene, featuring a young woman dressed in a teens era lingerie dress featuring "panniers," or flaps of fabric over the hips. $95.00 – 125.00.

Turn-of-the-century lingerie dresses were often elaborate but could also be quite simple.

A c.1904 – 1906 lingerie dress made of true muslin — a silky, almost gauze-like fabric. The sleeves, skirt, and bodice yoke are trimmed with lace inserts and the bodice and hip areas are shaped with tucks. The parasol is of ecru linen with a wooden handle and ivory tips. The belt and hat are reproductions. Dress, $95.00 – 175.00. Parasol, $100.00 – 180.00.

37

Two sets of drawers, c.1890s – 1908. The pair on the left is fine cotton trimmed with pintucking and machine- made lace. The pair on the right is heavier cotton trimmed with tucks and hand-crochet. $20.00 – 30.00.

"Aresco" label drawers from c.1900 – 1905, featuring lace trim and ribbon insertion. $25.00 – 30.00.

A young lady's lingerie dress from c. 1904 – 1907, featuring an embroidered and scalloped hemline and a puffed, "pigeon" front bodice. $95.00 – 140.00.

A lady posed for the photographer in a fine white dress, c.1900.

Typically turn-of-the-century lingerie, from a Victorian trade card.

Chapter Six
On Bridal Fashions

Bridal gowns continue to fascinate collectors. Perhaps this is because they are purely romantic; perhaps it's their carefully crafted stylishness — and perhaps it's simply because they are worn during such an important event as wedding nuptials, making them seem more intriguing than almost any other type of antique or vintage garment. But whatever the reason, while bridal gowns may be popular collectibles, there are many pitfalls in collecting them.

Not only do bridal gowns tend to be more costly than other gowns of the same period (because authentic bridal gowns are usually more rare), but they are often difficult to identify accurately. Amazingly, at antique markets and shows, I continue to see 1930s garden party-style dresses of flimsy materials trimmed with lace marked as Victorian wedding gowns. Too, I sometimes run across a person who wishes to sell or donate their mother's or grandmother's bridal dress, and even in this situation mistakes can be made. Just recently, a gentleman handed me what he called his mother's wedding dress from 1905 — but the one-piece, bias cut dress with a low, scooping neckline, and no sleeves (which never even saw the light of day in the early 1900s) was clearly from the 1930s. It is therefore my suggestion that before buying any gown marked as a bridal gown, you ask the seller the history behind the garment. Then make your own judgment.

The White Myth

Up until fairly recent years, most wedding gowns mirrored fashionable evening wear. Quite often it's impossible to distinguish between an authentic bridal gown and a white or cream evening gown unless you know the history behind the garment. Gowns from the early 1900s are particularly troublesome, since elaborate white gowns were popular in everyday wear, evening wear, and bridal wear. In fact, long before white was the color for wedding gowns, it was the color for confirmation, graduation, and debutante dresses — which were strikingly similar in style to bridal gowns. Fortunately, however, throughout most of history, there have been specific guidelines for being correct and suitable in bridal attire, so we have many clues to go by.

One vitally important clue to remember is that not all bridal gowns were white; though the first fashion plate of a white wedding gown appeared in 1813, it wasn't until the 1840s, when Queen Victoria wed Prince Albert, that the white wedding gown started to become popular. (Victoria, you might be interested to know, had the rare privilege of being one of the few women of her epoch allowed to propose to a man; it would have been considered unseemly for Albert — even though he was of royal lineage — to propose to a queen.) The lace alone on Victoria's gown took 200 people eight months to create; the seamstresses of the gown were sworn to keep the design a secret until the wedding event and were sequestered in a house in the country-side until the dress was completed.

The resulting gown, which became the dress every Victorian woman wished to wear to her wedding, was white satin with an 18-foot train and a white lace veil and trimmed with orange blossoms.

Now, Queen Victoria was never one to be an innovator, so some women did wear similar wedding outfits before her; Victoria, however, made them widely popular — and by 1860, etiquette books were saying things like: "The bride's dress must be of white entirely." For a church wedding at least. Unfortunately for collectors, bridesmaids also wore white gowns. This was such a sound tradition, in fact, that in 1883 one fashion magazine noted with surprise that "Quite a new departure has been taken recently in the adoption of colors for the dresses of bridesmaids instead of the repetition of the conventional white...."

Even so, there were many, many exceptions. As late as 1885 *Godey's Lady's Book* noted that navy blue and brown were especially popular color choices for bridal dresses — black could also be worn. Brides in mourning, widows, or older brides, often chose lavender. The Amherst Museum of New York, well known for its collection of wedding dresses, says few of their pre-1900 bridal dresses are white. In fact, one gown from 1870 is brilliant red taffeta and was worn by a school teacher.

Becoming a Sleuth

The best clue that a dress is a wedding gown is the presence of orange blossoms — the symbol of chastity and fertility. These might be of wax or silk, embroidered into the dress, or even woven into a lace pattern. Nevertheless, these will only be found on the gown of a wealthy women — someone who didn't need to find use for the gown after the wedding. As one turn-of-the-century etiquette book explained, "The wedding dress answers for an evening gown for three months, but if it is trimmed with orange blossoms, they must be replaced by white roses or other flowers." Yet even though orange blossoms had been considered the bridal flower in the nineteenth century, by the early twentieth century, some brides begged to differ. "Myrtle is most popular these days," one fashion magazine claimed.

Other clues may be found in the actual design of the dress. From the nineteenth century through the early 1900s, long sleeves and modest necklines were mandatory. In the 1920s, necklines tended still to be modest, but for the first time, short sleeve and even sleeveless styles were also worn. From the 1930s through the early 1960s, most bridal gowns had long sleeves, through necklines could scoop a little lower. Hemlines were always long — though in the 1920s (even though veils trailed the floor), skirts were fashionably short; later, in the 1960s, skirts would rise to knee level again. Trains were popular for bridal wear, but not mandatory, and up until the 1920s, trains were also worn in everyday evening attire.

In almost every case, the basic design of the bridal gown followed the same general lines of other fashionable dresses, but in 1939 when *Gone With The Wind* was released, some brides traded in the sleek lines of the era for gowns with nipped waists and ballooning skirts. In 1905 Butterick's *Dressmaking Up To Date* made a comment that should also be taken into consideration when trying to date a bridal gown. "Always choose the newest effect," the editors wrote, "since it is better to be a little in advance of the prevailing mode than even a trifle behind in this regard."

That same book also pointed to another difficulty for future collectors: "An evening dress may be high or low in the neck, as the wearer prefers, but a wedding gown must be high in the neck with long sleeves, although elbow sleeves are permissible with long gloves. If made with a yoke of lace attached to a guimpe, it may be detached, and the dress will afterward undergo early transition as a dinner or evening gown." Unlike most modern women, brides of the past usually expected that their bridal gown would have to be worn after the wedding. Often this meant lowering the neckline or changing the sleeve style, not to mention dyeing the entire dress, or layering a black or other-colored lace shell over it. In the November 1910 issue of *The Young Ladies' Journal*, one writer commented extensively about the fashions she saw at a recent wedding. "At first," she wrote after describing the bride's gown, "I thought Vera had been very extravagant, as I knew this kind of brocade costs a young fortune, but reflection told me it would wear forever, and might do duty on many white dresses before it was dyed and did duty in another tone." This sort of practicality is evident among brides right up to the 1930s, when Sears catalog featured a bridal gown of satin with slim, detachable sleeves worn under short puff sleeves; the long sleeves would have been worn for the wedding, but removed for the gown's reincarnation afterward. In most cases, it wasn't until the 1950s that most brides wore their wedding gown only once.

Ensuring Bridal History

For collectors, perchance one of the most important things to remember when collecting bridal gowns is to carefully guard any history you do discover behind the gown. If, for example, the dress belonged to your grandmother, your mother, or even yourself, take the time to have the original owner jot down this history of the dress: That it was their bridal gown, who they married, when they were married, and then carefully handstitch this note to the inside of the dress so that future collectors of the garment will know exactly where the dress came from and that it is, indeed, a true bridal gown. Someday, when someone else acquires the dress, they will be grateful.

Yet even while collectors must be mindful of many details when acquiring authentic bridal gowns, once found, no other piece of vintage clothing adds quite the same charm to a collection. As one Victorian writer put it: "There is something almost sacred about the bridal dress and veil, for the time when they are worn is the turning point in a woman's life, a new start is made and the future for her to make or mar stands before her."

The First Bridal Veil

While most pre-Queen Victoria brides wore wedding bonnets — not veils — the tradition of the bridal veil goes back to the ancients. Legend has it that in ancient Greece, in Sparta, one man's daughter, named Penelope, married Ulysses. Ulysses wanted to leave Sparta and move to another city. The father wanted them to stay in Sparta. So Ulysses told his wife, "You can answer this request; it is yours to determine whether you will remain with your father in Sparta, or depart with your husband; you are mistress to the decision." According to Godey's Lady's Book, which retold the story in 1831, "The beautiful Penelope, finding herself in this dilemma, blushed, and, without making the least reply, drew the veil over her face, thereby intimating a denial of her father's request, and sank into the arms of her husband."

The bridal veil made entirely of lace also has ancient origins, and, interestingly enough, the word "lace" comes from the Latin word "laqueare," meaning to snare. The American term "lasso" is also derived from the same stem.

This magnificent two-piece bridal gown is an exquisite rendering of tucks, trim, fabric, and detail. The fabric is richly corded with insets of pintucked silk and ruching. The fitted bodice, slim sleeves, and dainty sleeve epaulets date the gown to c. 1897. $450.00 – 1,000.00.
Courtesy of Persona Vintage Clothing.

A two-piece dress, c.1858 – 1863. The boned bodice has a hook and eye front closure, and pagoda sleeves with attached undersleeves. It was purchased with the hoops on page 22, plus a plain white petticoat of the same period, trimmed only with narrow sawtooth edging at the hem and a single initial embroidered in royal blue on the waistband. The set is purported to be a bride's wedding costume. Set, $400.00 – 500.00.

The inner sleeve of the dress features pleated trim, and the undersleeves are daintily embellished.

This c.1968-1969 heavy satin bridal dress imitates the styles of the early 1800s, with a raised empire waistline, short puffed sleeves, and a velvet ribbon for "something blue." $30.00 – 75.00.

Photo courtesy of the Lassiter/Cheetham collection.

A two-piece gown worn for a 1900 wedding. $175.00 – 275.00.

Photo courtesy of the Lassiter/Cheetham collection.

Photo courtesy of Karen Augusta.

A c.1840s bridal gown of fine muslin trimmed with white hand embroidery. $400.00 – 900.00.

Photo courtesy of Allan and Barbara King.

An all-over lace gown from the early 1900s, purported to be a bridal dress. $100.00 – 300.00.

Photo courtesy of the Lassiter/Cheetham collection.

An 1856 wedding gown of wool challis. The only reason it can be definitely pinpointed as a bridal dress is because its provenance is known; it was worn by Elizabeth Thompson of New Braintree, Massachusetts. $400.00 – 500.00.

Photo courtesy of Karen Augusta.

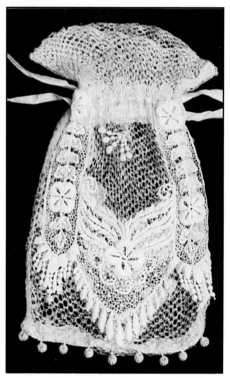

A c.1900 – 1905 "wedding purse" of crocheted silk. $30.00 – 75.00.

47

Chapter Seven
The Love Of A Bonnet

"The room was like a waving field of feathers," Richard Rush, America's minister to England in 1818, wrote. "Some blue like the sky, some tinged with red, here you saw violet and yellow, there shades of green, but the most were pure white like a tuft of snow." With their flirtatious waving and bouncing, it was easy to see why women's plumed hats were so massively popular. And yet in the early 1800s, hats themselves were a fairly new adornment for women. Before the late seventeenth century, women donned only skimpy mob caps; it wasn't until the nineteenth century that women turned hats it into an eminently feminine fashion.

By the 1840s, when women began wearing bonnets, one or two plumes were all that seemed appropriate for a lady. A sort of compromise between the old-fashioned mob cap and the "fast" masculine-inspired hat, the bonnet was a strange contraption of wooden slats and fabric. Quite different from anything men had ever worn, the bonnet soon became the epitome of femininity. So much so, in fact, that Julia Grant (wife of the Civil War general soon to be President) claimed it saved lives. In her autobiography, she recounts that when she and several other members of President Lincoln and General Grant's entourage were boating down the James River during the war, sharpshooters were spotted along the shoreline. Well within shooting range, Julia was understandably alarmed. But Admiral Porter soothed her by reassuring, "These Southern fellows are all too gallant. They would not fire on a boat with women in it. These ladies' bonnets will protect us." Since no one was shot at, he was apparently right.

For informal wear, women continued to wear trifling caps of gauzy fabric trimmed with delicate lace and ribbon. Even young, unmarried women donned these, though today we might consider them matronly. In fact, at the time they were considered far

from homely (in 1844, one cap was dubbed "The Bonnet Assassin" — and apparently, it lived up to its name, making "a tolerably pretty woman look very killing").

Millinery Modes

In the 1860s, the reign of the bonnet began to crumble. It started quite innocently, when Madame Worth (wife of Charles Worth, the famous couture designer) ventured into town wearing a bonnet that, unlike all other bonnets previous to it, had no "modesty piece" to hide the back of the neck. "I never saw anything so perfectly disgusting," cried one society woman. "That hat is simply indecent." Still, one of Worth's most influential clients, Princess Metternich, thought the style charming and quickly adopted the fashion for herself. Other slaves of fashion soon followed her example.

The bonnet continued to become more brief as the nineteenth century progressed. At first not allowing a woman's profile to be seen (hence the old saying about so-called "masculine" women: "You can see her nose beyond her bonnet"), the newest bonnets revealed even the daintiest of profiles. As early as 1851 "Seaside Hats" (those wide-brimmed, floppy hats Scarlet O'Hara favored) rivaled the bonnet. "Considered rather fast after the long reign of the meek bonnet," the hat nonetheless began to take over the throne of millinery. Still, wide-brimmed hats were the exception — the rule being a small, pillbox-like hat trimmed frivolously. By 1867, *The Saturday Review* was complaining about this new fashion. "It is long enough since a bonnet meant shelter to the face or protection to the head," feminist journalist Lynn Linton wrote. "That fragment of a bonnet which at present (is fashionable) is ornamented with birds, portions of beasts, reptiles, and insects. We have seen a 'bonnet' composed of a rose and a couple of feathers, another of two or three butterflies or as many beads and a bit of lace, and a third represented by five green leaves joined at the stalks." The modern age of millinery had begun (even if people were reluctant to call the new feminine hat a "hat" and insisted upon referring to it as a "bonnet" — although it didn't resemble a bit the old-fashioned sunshade).

"A bonnet is simply an excuse for a feather, a pretext for a spray of flowers, the support for an aigrette, the fastening for a plume of Russian cocks' feathers," Charles Blanc, author of the 1877 volume *Art & Ornament in Dress* insisted. "It is placed on the head not to protect it, but that it may be seen better. Its great use is to be charming." Few women disagreed. *Godey's Lady's Book* put it thusly: "A young lady who lately gave an order to a milliner for a bonnet, said: 'You are to make it plain, but at the same time smart, as I sit in a conspicuous place in church.'" Millinery had become a sort of social indicator.

This Julia Grant also commented on. It seems that occasionally a woman would attend her White House receptions without a bonnet, "which would indicate that she was one of the receiving party." This situation was handled firmly by the First Lady. "This little maneuver was never repeated by the same person," she wrote.

Of course, there were those who wished such social symbols as the bonnet would quietly disappear. One Mormon man complained in the 1870s that "our women want new bonnets." This wouldn't be such a terrible thing except that "all this finery is costly; yet a man who loves his wives can hardly refuse to dress them as they see other ladies dress. To clothe one woman is as much as most men in America can afford. In the good old times, an extra wife cost a man little or nothing. She wore a calico sunshade which she made herself. Now she must have a bonnet. A bonnet costs twenty dollars and implies a shawl and gown to match. A bonnet to one wife, with shawl and gown to match, implies the like to every other wife...." A predicament, indeed.

"Could there be a more exact instance of 'How Not To Do It' than by placing such an article on a human head?" the dress reform journal *Dress* pointed out in 1888. "The object covering the head is to protect the eyes from too much

light or from rain and to keep the sun from beating on the back of the head. A bonnet usually leaves both back and forehead bare, and adds the discomfort of having to carry a (parasol) which is always a strain on the back from the position required by the arm. The strings of the bonnet huddle up the throat, so that the wearer can only turn her head partially and with difficulty."

Indeed, some millinery concoctions were so bizarre that one can only assume milliners frequently laughed behind their customers' backs. "On hats and bonnets," one 1885 fashion magazine advised, tongue-in-cheek, "include not only those insects and birds which appeal to our sense of beauty but those which cause a revulsion of feeling such as spider, water-beetles, caterpillars, and even lizards and toads." A year later, *Lady's World* reported, quite seriously, about the latest trend: "On some of the sealskin toques and hats are to be seen tiny cubs of bears, or baby squirrels, which seem to be playing hide and seek among the wings and bows."

Still, feathers (and even whole birds) continued to be the favorite millinery trimming. So much so that many species of birds were in danger of extinction. In 1885, New Jersey felt it necessary to pass a law forbidding the killing of any non-game birds. Other states soon followed their example, and when the National Audubon Society was founded in 1886, one of their primary objectives was "to prevent, as far as possible...the wearing of feathers as ornament or trimming for dress."

Suffragette Savvy

Yet by the turn of the century, hats — befeathered or not — were a dominating feature in women's fashions. In the nineteenth century, hats — not bonnets — had always symbolized emancipation for women: first when adopted during the Civil War (when the feminist movement really began), then again when revived as suffragettes were heading toward the battle lines. As woman's emancipation became more widespread, so did her hats. Brims grew to great proportions — sometimes surpassing shoulder width. "To say the hats of the present season are large does not begin to express it. They are huge...," *McCall's* noted in 1908. Young women now wore only hats; bonnets with ties were left to children and matrons. "Hats with a chin strap attachment look very much like they were intended to keep the wearer's mouth shut," Carrie Hall wrote in her reminiscences. "If the real reason — if any — for using the chin strap is ever known, this guess may not be so far wrong."

As women threw out their chin straps, the popularity of noticeably long hatpins surged. Interestingly, though hatpins had been around since mid-century, men took sudden exception to those long, pointed devices; suddenly hatpins seemed to take on new meaning. In 1913 New Orleans passed a law banning hatpins with noticeable points — and the police were instructed to enforce the law strictly. "It is no joke to watch those shining points and then approach the owner and warn her," one officer admitted. Some women reportedly attacked police with their pins — an action readily attributed to all suffragettes, whether they had ever done the deed or not.

Still, women themselves were not always madly in love with hats. In 1907 when actress Sarah Bernhardt purchased her own theatre, she immediately banned hats because they made viewing the stage — and the actress upon it — difficult. Even fashion magazines found little good to say about hats during some seasons. Other women expressed an abhorrence for hats because they were grotesque or ugly — and simply because they were a hassle to wear. "I hated the veils that, worn twisted into a squiggle under my chin, dotted my vision with huge spots like symptoms of liver trouble. They flattened even my short eyelashes," one fashionable young woman of the turn of the century wrote.

But the vast majority of women clung to their hats adoringly. To buy a new piece of millinery was considered one of the greatest treats money could buy. *Godey's Lady's Book* (always understanding such matters) reported on this phenomenon as early as the 1860s. "A young lady — a sensible girl — gives the following catalog of different kinds of love," they wrote. "'The sweetest, a mother's love; the longest, a brother's love; the strongest, a woman's love; the dearest, a man's love; the sweetest, longest, strongest, dearest love — a love of a bonnet.'"

The Rise (and Fall) of Modern Hats

Yet by the 1920s, the bonnet, like all things Victorian, was passé. The modern girl wore a "bob hat" over her bobbed hair — a cap called a cloche. Though the basic style was simple, the cloche was anything but. The old Victorian trappings were still intact: large flowers, ruching, embroidery, lace, and beading all adorned the flapper's hat.

Women clung to cloches until about 1939 when a Victorian resurgence came into vogue. Wide-brims garnished with veilings and flowers were cherished — but more importantly, truly new millinery styles emerged. Perhaps because clothing was restricted and severe because of World War II, accessories — especially hats — were frivolous, fantastical, and wild. "The way not to look this year," *Vogue* instructed in 1945, "is hard, sharp, cold, even bold…It's out because the men can't bear it. The new hats are…Lady Hats." *The Millinery Trade Review* also put their two-cents in: "Hats after V-J day must be optimistic, homecoming hats to greet the boys. They must be exciting, new, (and) free from foreign influence…."

"Notwithstanding the continued practice of going bareheaded, best taste exacts that a hat be worn with street clothes in all cities whether day time or night," Emily Post insisted in the early 1950s. Yet hats were becoming passé, No one really knows why. After all, hats and head-coverings had been worn by women since ancient times. Perhaps it was that women had become accustomed to going hatless in the lean war years. Some writers have also speculated that it was a woman's new, more independent role in the world that made her doff her hat — but this seems unlikely, since men still wore hats. More likely, it was the milliner herself who brought hats to their demise; hats of the late 1940s and early 1950s often lacked uniqueness — and were frequently nothing less than ridiculous. Certainly designers did continue to include hats in their collections (just as they do today), but the average woman was most often seen without one.

Hedda Hopper, Hollywood gossip queen and well-known hat-lover, had her own theory. "The milliners, especially the males, have helped stitch glamour's shroud," she wrote. "Deep inside whatever they call their souls, they hate women. They made the most ridiculous concoctions for women to wear on their heads. Hats like table doilies, little potholders, coal scuttles, dishpans, crash helmets, bedpans. Husbands were ignored when they complained, 'Where in God's name did you get that thing? Whoever made it must hate your sex.' Not until other women laughed at them did the glamour pusses discard their psychotic chapeaux and go bareheaded. By then the designers had ruined their own racket; they'd killed the sale of hats."

But whatever the case, hats are now a popular and rich source for collectors. Though Victorian hats have grown increasingly impossible to find in good condition and at an affordable price (especially turn-of-the-century wide-brims laden with feathers), hats from the 1920s forward are inexpensive and fun. Today, we don't wear hats unless we want to stand out from the crowd — so vintage hats, even if they are "psychotic," are a joy.

Tips For Dating Hats

1. If the hat has a label that is glued on, it dates to the 1920s or later. Still, just because your hat has a label that's sewn-in doesn't mean it's pre-1920s. Even today, well-made hats have sewn-in labels.

2. If the hat possesses a designer's label, it is usually fairly easy to pinpoint an era for the hat. Look for the designer's advertisements in fashion magazines, or consult a good book on hats, such as Women's Hats of the 20th Century *and* Vintage Hats & Bonnets *(see the bibliography/recommended reading for more information on these books and others).*

3. All straw hats were created by hand until the early 1900s when straw-sewing machines were invented.

4. Some styles have been revived repeatedly — the pillbox, for example. In the twentieth century, it first appeared in the teens and was dubbed a "toque." It tended to be well-embellished, and it was big — big enough to fit over the full, all-hair-on-top-of-the-head hairdos of the era. In the late 1950s, the pillbox returned in a more plain and much smaller form — it perched atop the head rather precariously. Other styles that have been revived in the twentieth century include the cloche, first worn in the 1920s, but revived in the 1960s and the wide-brim "picture" hat, first worn in the early 1900s, then in the early 1920s, again in the late 1930s and early 1940s, and, finally, in the 1950s.

5. Often, the way experts date hats is by feel: How old does the fabric look? Is the beading glass, plastic, jet, or some other material? Is the veil made of synthetic materials or silk?, etc...making it difficult to explain to others how to date a hat. The best way to learn to date hats is through study. Books with both period fashion illustrations and modern photos of old hats are helpful, but if you can manage to find a local museum with a collection of hats that has been dated by an expert, take advantage of this wonderful learning opportunity. You might also seek out a local vintage clothing dealer who knows a bit about hats; this way, you might be able to actually handle some hats and hear what she has to say about why she feels a particular hat dates to a particular period.

Women's millinery from an early 1900s fashion plate. $10.00 – 25.00.

A turn-of-the-century hat featuring a plethora of feathers and bunches of fake grapes. It is constructed of beaver, a popular material for hats in the early 1900s. $75.00 – 125.00.

In the late 1930s and early 1940s, Scarlett O'Hara-style broad-brims were popular. $25.00 – 50.00.

Frivolously feathered hats like this one date to the 1950s. $20.00 – 40.00.

Photo Courtesy of Karen Augusta.

This straw bonnet trimmed with ribbon and lace dates to c.1830. $200.00 – 400.00.

A natural straw hat in the modified cloche style of the 1930s. $25.00 – 45.00.

Photo Courtesy of Karen Augusta.

A girlish bonnet from c. 1900 – 1920. $25.00 – 45.00.

A taffeta bonnet and cape set purportedly worn over the Oregon Trail in the 1850s. The bonnet brim is stiffened with wooden slats. With provenance $95.00 – 175.00. Without provenance $75.00 – 95.00.

Romantically styled broad-brims like this were worn in the early 1920s.

Courtesy of Old Friends.

A 1920s cloche featuring braid trim and embroidery. $30.00 – 65.00.

A mourning cap from the second half of the nineteenth century, fashioned from lace and millinery wire. Victorians had specific rules about clothing worn during mourning; pure black (usually crepe) was worn during the first stage of mourning, then a white collar and sleeve cuffs could be added. Only in the final stages of mourning could colors — purple, lavender, or gray — be used to trim otherwise black attire. $45.00 – 85.00.

Fuchsia was *the* fashion color of the 1930s and early 1940s. This 1940s hat is no exception, from its wings to its veil. $40.00 – 65.00.

Photo courtesy of Karen Augusta.

A c.1860 "spoon" bonnet of woven and pleated straw and horsehair. $200.00 – 400.00.

Large pillboxes (traditionally called toques) like this one of satin with braid and flower trim were sometimes worn during 1910 – 1920. $40.00 – 65.00. Courtesy of Old Friends.

A 1920s hat trimmed with ribbon, flowers, and braid trim. $25.00 – 60.00.
Courtesy of Old Friends.

Courtesy of Old Friends.

A plumed hat from the early 1900s. $95.00 – 150.00.

Courtesy of Old Friends.

This 1930 hat is reminiscent of late Victorian hats. The large hatpin is purely decorative and permanently attached to the hat. $20.00 – 35.00.

Courtesy of Old Friends.

A marabou feather hat from the late 1950s – early 1960s. $30.00 – 65.00.

Photo courtesy of Karen Augusta.

A c.1850s straw bonnet with a proper "modesty piece." $200.00 – 350.00.

This broad-brim trimmed with fabric, flowers, and feathers would have been quite fashionable in the early 1900s. $150.00 – 275.00.

In the 1940s, hats were often colorful. $20.00 – 30.00.

Chapter Eight
Those Neo-Victorians

Collectors — from novices to museum curators — sometimes lose sight of the fact that trends in fashion are about as consistent as a weatherman's predictions. But think about it; have you adopted all the current vogues into your current wardrobe? Probably not. And neither did the women of the past.

Nowhere are modes and sub-modes more varied, it seems, than in the twentieth century. So it is not surprising to me when an enthusiast shows off a "Victorian" dress from her collection and it actually turns out to be from the 1940s. How could anyone confuse such a relatively modern dress with a Victorian toilette? People do it all the time.

Some mislabeling of twentieth century dresses comes purely from a lack of understanding about historic styles. More times than I care to count I have seen typically 1930s garden party type dresses dated to the Victorian era — by both collectors and dealers.

But sometimes enthusiasts are more justifiably confused; some authentic twentieth century dresses are decidedly Victorian. For instance, the dress pictured below left has a great many elements of Victorian fashion: a beautifully woven wool skirt, a velvet bodice with wooden buttons, even a "bustle." But the dress dates to the late 1940s. How to tell?

- Hint #1: The bodice is free from any boning (which is unusual in Victorian bodices in general and almost never seen in bustle-era Victorian bodices).
- Hint #2: The bodice is not interlined (as almost all Victorian bodices are).
- Hint #3: There is not a "stay tape" or belt on the inside of the waist (which was used in most post-1870, pre-1900 bodices).
- Hint #4: The skirt is neither interlined nor features any velvet, braid, horsehair, or crinoline hem binding (which are found on virtually all Victorian skirts).
- Hint #5: Such large, wooden buttons would be rare on a Victorian dress.

But, you say, the dress just doesn't look 1940s? Though it wasn't a universally accepted style, neo-Victorian dresses were worn from c.1947 – 1949 as a softened look emerged in women's fashions. And the look wasn't only for the frivolously wealthy, either. A peek inside the ever down-to-earth Sears catalog details this:

"The 'Back Look' is the Newest Look..."
"New Bustle Back Suits..."
"Simply wonderful, any way you look at it. Straight, slim front...rippling, bustle back... marvelous profile...."

Sears' headlines — not to mention those in fashion magazines like *Vogue* and *Harper's Bazaar* — raved about the new, decidedly feminine Victorian style.

Other eras hosted their own brands of neo-Victorianism, too. Quite unusual (and somewhat rare) are dresses from the 1930s with that "pioneer" Victorian style, which actually foretold many spin-off styles that

Dress described on page 62.

Dress description on page 63.

appeared in the 1940s and 1950s.

The dress pictured on the left is made of lightweight plaid taffeta in colorful green and red shades. The general line of the dress dates it to the late 1930s or very early 1940s, but the gathered hemline trimmed with lace and a velvet ribbon gives it a feminine, Victorian look rarely associated with the period. But check out some issues of *Harper's Bazaar* or *Vogue* from c.1939, and you'll see unquestionably neo-Victorian styles gracing some of the pages.

Perhaps better recognized are c.1920 dresses in the pannier, bustle, or hoopskirt style. A desperate attempt by fabric manufacturers to make fashions more fabric-consuming (and a flash-in-the-pan style that received faint welcome), such designs were most often seen in evening wear. They often feature boning (to shape the skirt, if not the bodice), but reveal themselves as twentieth century concoctions with their spaghetti straps or relatively short skirts. "They are doing their best to turn women back into the former restless search for beauty amid wasp waists, balloon skirts, trains, and draperies," one period writer commented. "The campaign was on," another woman wrote about the phenomenon; "flaring, flaunting, flower-beds of skirts, displayed in shop windows, were to tempt the shopper."

Most widely known are the neo-Victorian styles popularized by Parisian designer Christian Dior around 1947. Yearning for the elegance of the fashions he remembered his mother wearing, Dior launched his "New Look" campaign with corseted waists, padded bosoms and hips, plastic hoopskirts, and Gibson Girl style shirtwaists. "From the era of Madame Bovary," *Vogue* described the New Look fashions, "wasp-waisted Gibson Girl shirtwaists, pleated or tucked...slow-sloped, easy shoulders...wrapped and bound middles...long, deeply shaped shadow box décolleté...padded hips...." The New Look woman was swathed in Victorian style.

Some "New Look" garments can easily be confused with the Victorian fashions they emulate, if they are not carefully examined; many Victorian construction methods were revived on the best New Look garments, and at first blush, all the Victorian trappings seem present: stay tapes (ribbon belts that fasten inside the garment at the waistline), interlinings, piping, even boning, padding, and hem bindings.

If a garment label is present, it will clue savvy collectors into the fact that the article is twentieth century garb. (Some Victorian dresses have labels, but they are rare and do not have the modern wording or typefaces seen on twentieth century labels.) Otherwise, careful attention should be paid to hem lengths (with the exception of some evening gowns, they'll be shorter), padding at the hips (which was never built into Victorian skirts), lightly padded shoulders (never used in Victorian fashions), and synthetic fabrics.

Undoubtedly the height of neo-Victorian style was the 1950s; it was a time when nearly every woman wore some neo-Victorian article, fashions slightly subdued from the New Look. With full skirts (now nearly always supported by "crinoline" net petticoats and not by New Look plastic hoopskirts), fitted bodices, parasols, and gloves, the fashions of the 1950s are the most popular of the neo-Victorian styles among today's collector; nonetheless, some people mistake certain 1950s garments (some evening gowns in particular) with nineteenth century designs. For the record:

- Crinoline or net underskirts were never attached to Victorian skirts.
- Arched hemlines (that is, hems that rise slightly in front, making walking easier) were not generally worn in the Victorian era.
- Fuller hips were achieved through separate garments worn under clothing during the Victorian era; skirts and bodices were never actually padded at the hips.
- Strapless dresses never saw the light of day in the nineteenth century.
- Spaghetti straps are a twentieth century contrivance.

They might be a rarely discussed subject among vintage fashion collectors, but neo-Victorian fashions offer many exciting collecting opportunities. For those who love the elegance and beauty of Victorian fashions but have trouble working them into their budget, twentieth century neo-Victorian designs offer a stimulating alternative. And for those who thrive on the classic lines of post 1920 fashions, neo-Victorian styles add diversity and an unusual aspect to a collection of twentieth century fashions.

Rarely acknowledged today, neo-Victorians are generally more accessible: a collector's treasure-trove.

This plastic hoop skirt was manufactured by one of the most popular makers of such skirts. A 1949 ad in *Glamour* magazine praised the "Belle-o-the-Ball," noting correctly that it "adjusts to any size, including BUSTLE and FATHINGALE effects. Opens to a 90" skirt — folds to only 8" for packing and easy traveling...." $40.00 – 75.00.
Courtesy of Lydia's Timeless Accessories.

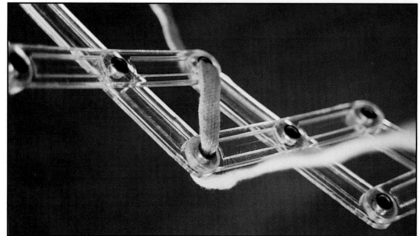

The 1949 *Glamour* ad also noted that the hoops came "complete with rich plastic carrying case that doubles as extra make-up kit with handy compartment for accessories."

This dress from the 1940s has many Victorian-inspired elements, most notably, a bustle effect. $30.00 – 50.00.

Two dresses from the early 1940s; one is from an ad, the other is an existing collectible — but both harken back to turn-of-the-century "pioneer" clothing, and both are fashioned out of plaid taffeta and lace trim. Collectible plaid dress, $20.00 – 30.00.

At first glance, this might appear to be a Victorian dress: the corseted, tight-fitting waist and bustle skirt harken back to the 1870s and 1880s. But in actuality, this is a 1950s evening gown.

Hoop and pannier revivals from 1920.

Chapter Nine
Men Do It, Too

Although this book focuses on women's fashions (because women make up the majority of historical fashion collectors), it's perfectly legal for men to be vintage fashion enthusiasts, too. Fashions for men today are so similar to each other (some say they're boring), it's no wonder many men get a kick out of collecting the more variable (more interesting?) clothes of the past. Some men even collect women's fashions (though their Monday night football buddies may not realize it). And why shouldn't men be just as thrilled with the history behind clothes as women are.

Take heart, men. Though you may be a minority in the fashion collecting world, you are in good company. Just think of all the men whose interest in the fashions and society of the past have led them to re-enact such important events in history as the Civil War. Remember, too, that until recently, most experts in the field of costume (including women's dress) were men, including the still revered writers and

experts C. Willet Cunnington and James Laver. In more recent years, masculine experts in the field, such as Richard Martin and Harold Koda, have acted as curators for one of the world's most outstanding collections of fashions at the Metropolitan Museum of Art.

Though the history of men's clothes is, for the most part, a little less complicated than the history of women's, collecting guidelines are the same: Find out what eras interest you, buy representative garments and/or make reproductions of them, and care for them well.

An early twentieth century morning coat of bottle green wool; it has a matching shawl collar vest and is worn with striped gray trousers. The silk top hat is collapsible for traveling. The woman's dress is 1913 – 1914.
Coat, $65.00 – 95.00.
Vest, $20.00 – 40.00.
Trousers, $40.00 – 65.00.
Hat, $85.00 – 150.00.
Dress, $45.00 – 85.00.

Courtesy of the Lassiter/Cheetham collection; photo by Steve Falconer.

A dapper young man of the 1890s dressed to impress in a silk top hat, cane, and fashionable suit.

Courtesy of the Lassiter/Cheetham collection; photo by Steve Falconer.

This handsome couple is attired for the evening; the man's tailcoat and trousers are from the early twentieth century and are worn with a formal vest of white cotton brocade. Tailcoat and trousers, $50.00 – 80.00 ea. Vest, $20.00 – 40.00.

A brother and sister attired for an 1890s holiday.

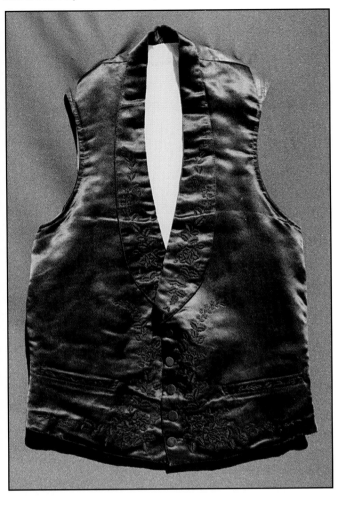

A c.1850s man's vest of black satin with embroidered accents. $45.00 – 75.00.

A "Prince Albert" style frock coat from 1902 – 1905; its flared, mid-calf length imitated the styles of the 1840s. Coat, $65.00 – 95.00. Hat, $35.00 – 75.00.

A man in the everyday attire of the late 1880s – 1890s.

Chapter Ten
Tokens Of Innocence

"Take this white venture for a token of innocence...." So men of the cloth said in the sixteenth century, already noting the christening gown as a vital part of the christening ceremony. Fussed over and carefully created, it seems only natural that the intricately constructed, elaborately embellished christening gown is now a favorite among collectors. But there is more to collecting these delicate articles than may at first meet the eye.

Few collectors will be fortunate enough to uncover gowns from before the early 1800s. In fact, most collectors of christening gowns actually prefer gowns that date to at least the mid-nineteenth century since before that time they usually weren't the pure white, ornate little garments we think of today. Cotton gowns are most frequently found in today's market, silk being rare to find in good condition. And condition is everything in the world of christening gowns. Too many excellent condition gowns still exist today to make even the slightest stain or tear acceptable in the eyes of most collectors.

The Dating Game

One of the most difficult aspects of collecting christening gowns is dating them. Even today, antique and vintage designs are re-created by doting grandmothers and aunts. In the past, christenings gowns were often passed down from generation to generation, sometimes being revamped to suit more modern tastes. Flounces were added to hems, short sleeves were made long, long skirts were made shorter, and sometimes most of the original antique lace was removed. Therefore, careful inspection is an essential part of dating christening gowns.

The general style lines of the gown can be helpful in many cases — though they won't necessarily help you to discern whether or not the garment is a true christening gown. True christening gowns almost always have long skirts — in the Victorian era, many skirts were at least four feet long; the wealthy often favored skirts that were long enough so that when the mother held the child, the gown would fall all the way to her own hem. It wasn't until the 1920s that shorter skirts became popular, usually no longer than three feet. Nonetheless, the occasional short Victorian christening gown does pop up; some were shortened in the nineteenth century, but others appear to have originated in the shorter style. If you're uncertain whether the dress is a true christening gown rather than just a child's special occasion dress, check the length between the waistline and the sleeve-hole. A measurement of some four to five inches indicates it was, indeed, designed for a baby. As a final indicator, note the type of fabric. If it is very fine (often gauzy-looking) cotton or silk, it is quite probably a christening gown. Less flimsy fabrics were usually used for everyday clothes.

Christening gowns from the nineteenth century usually feature short sleeves; rather low, scooping necklines; fitted waistlines; and a seam between the bodice and the skirt. Rarely were skirts hemmed in a traditional manner but instead featured a lace or eyelet edging. Before about 1890, christening gowns were most often designed to look like open-fronted robes worn over a skirt. Therefore, "robings" (which look something like revers on a suit), well trimmed with lace, embroidery, or some other form of embellishment, may be an indicator that the piece is pre-1890s.

By the turn of the century, robings were used far less frequently and other more modern design elements became popular. Several rows of flounces running all the way around the skirt usually indicates the gown dates to the late 1890s or early 1900s. Bodice yokes usually date from the 1890s through the teens. Longer sleeves were favored from about the late 1890s to the

1930s. After the 1930s, styles were far more arbitrary, and many antique and vintage style elements became popular (as is true even today). Sometimes the general feel of the garment can indicate its age. The Art Deco movement that so drastically changed women's fashions in the 1920s, for example, also had an effect on christening gowns; the soft curves popular at the turn of the century were frequently exchanged for geometric lines. Gowns from the 1920s through 1930s also tend to be less suffocated by laces and flounces.

It's In the Details

The construction of the garment is also an important consideration. Well-made gowns are, for obvious reasons, preferred by collectors, and while most christening gowns were created by careful, loving hands, certain methods of construction and sewing can help collectors pinpoint the garment's date of origin. For instance, gowns from the first 40 years of the nineteenth century are always entirely handsewn, though the stitches may be so regular and fine they may fool an eye unfamiliar with such precise handsewing. For this reason, it's a good idea to examine the stitching with a magnifying glass. If adjoining stitches seem to come out the same hole, they were stitched with a sewing machine, unless the stitches on the underside overlap, which indicates the seam was handstitched with a technique called backstitching. However, christening gowns from almost any period might be handstitched, even if the sewing machine was favored by most people for everyday sewing after the 1840s.

Victorian christening gowns will be as beautiful on the inside as they are on the outside. Every seam will be handfinished — very often with the raw edges of the fabric turned toward each other and handstitched closed. Tapes or ribbons often gather the necklines and waists of gowns from the Victorian era — making them ideal to pass down to other babies who might be a smaller or larger size. Some gowns from the 1880s through the teens also have small openings in the back, absent of fastenings; these were included so that the mother could hold the baby comfortably without wrinkling the christening gown. Up to the 1920s or so, all buttonholes were handworked, and buttons were frequently mother-of-pearl, though in the early 1900s, crocheted buttons were extremely popular. Still, buttons on christening gowns didn't appear until about the 1870s; gowns before this time were closed with ties running down the back. From time to time, gowns are found without any indication of fastenings. This style was used up through the 1870s; small, decorative pins originally held the garment closed.

So whether your fascination with these dainty gowns lends itself toward the sentimental vintage or the handsewn antique, whether the gown is a work of art acquired from an estate auction or a family heirloom passed down, christening gowns are a unique and timeless treasure. Trimmed with yards of lace and featuring the tiniest, cutest of sleeves, christening gowns are much more than a "token of innocence;" they are a celebration of the precious bundles who once donned them.

The baby shown in this 1898 fashion plate wears an elaborate cloak and bonnet, appropriate for a christening.

A christening gown from the early 1900s. It is fashioned from white cotton and features tiny hand-crocheted buttons and French seams. $65.00 – 100.00.

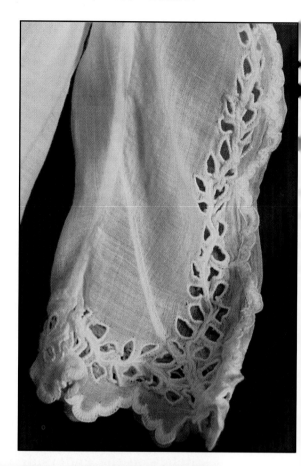

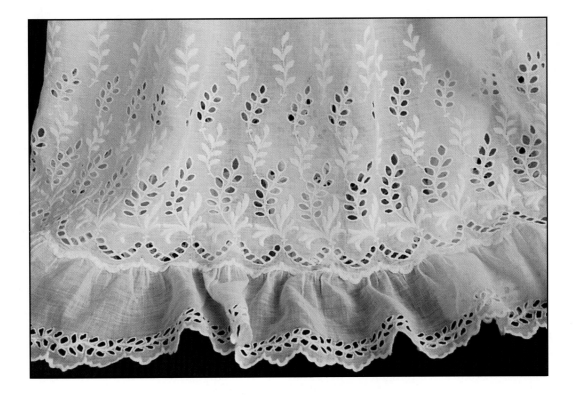

This christening gown dates to the turn of the century and features beautiful lace insets. $150.00 – 190.00.

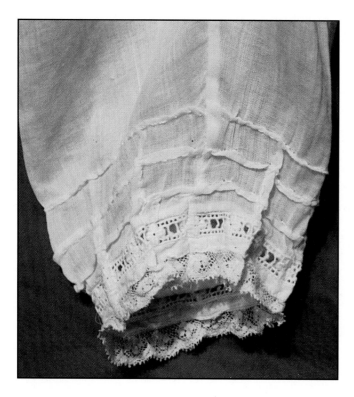

Found under both arms, these delicate pleats give shape to the gowns.

A batiste christening gown trimmed with Valenciennes lace.

Chapter Eleven
Children's Clothing

The field of children's fashions covers such vast territory — from teenager's clothing, to toddler's clothes, to baby's clothes, to one of the most popular single areas of children's fashions: christening gowns — that it is difficult to write a book on the subject, let alone condense the information into a single chapter. But my intent in writing this chapter isn't to give a thorough presentation of the subject but to open your eyes (if they aren't already) to the many wonderful possibilities available to collectors of children's garb.

Babies' clothes of all types are especially popular among today's collectors; there is something too sweet about tiny garments with miniscule sleeves to make baby clothes an easy thing to pass up for most collectors. One of the benefits of collecting baby clothes is that they are readily available, even in antique shows or stores that don't usually carry antique and vintage clothing. Often, too, baby clothes are in terrific condition, because they've been fondly stored in family trunks for years.

Clothing for toddlers or older children is a bit harder to come by, partly because fewer dealers tend to carry it and partly because they seem to have been less frequently saved by their original owners. Nonetheless, many lovely garments for boys and girls from this age group exist, particularly in the area of special occasion wear.

Most fashion collectors have some teenagers' clothing in their collection, whether they realize it or not. It is usually impossible (without some record of who wore the garment and when) to prove that any given garment is a teenag-

er's, but there are some clues that sway the facts in that direction. One is the size of the garment. Most teenagers' garments, whether for a young man or woman, are petite. I have also found that rather trendy garments (like the bodice on page 131) are frequently quite small; this tends to make me believe they may have been worn by teenagers for their debuts or some other very important coming-out style party.

Slightly more difficult to find, unless they are for babies, are children's accessories. Fans, hats, purses, parasols, shoes, and related items are a pleasant find and are often just as elaborate as their adult counterparts; the only difference is usually the size of the accessory.

But whatever type of children's fashions catches your eye and cries "take me home!," whether it is a nineteenth century boy's sailor suit, a girl's 1920s cloche hat, or a baby's knitted bootie, you're likely to get

Tiny felt baby slippers, trimmed with wool and one-quarter inch buttons. $10.00 – 30.00.
Courtesy of Vintage Silhouettes.

hooked. I never thought I'd collect children's clothes until somebody gave me a turn-of-the-century christening gown, followed by a nine-teenth century girl's velvet dress. They tugged at my heart strings, and I haven't been the same collector since.

A brother and sister from the 1920s.

This boy is dressed in typically early 1900s attire: a large straw hat and a suit with a long belted jacket and short knickers.

Children's clothing was barely mentioned in most fashion magazines until the mid-nineteenth century, and color fashion plates rarely featured only children's clothing until the 1870s. This plate is from an 1870s issue of *The Metropolitan.* $25.00 – 35.00.

Pretty Summer Frocks
DESCRIBED ON PAGE 40
JULY, 1902

A 1905 fashion plate from *The Delineator*. $20.00 – 30.00.

CHILDREN'S FASHIONS FOR JUNE.

Girls' dresses from the June 1864 issue of *Godey's Lady's Book.*

Chapter Twelve
Fabulous Fashion Plates

In 1770, the world of fashion looked upon a thin, wordy journal dubbed *The Ladies' Magazine* with shock and delight. Featuring a simple, black and white line drawing of a fashionable Parisian gown, the magazine had invented the soon to be cherished tradition of fashion plates. From the late eighteenth century through the 1930s, fashion plates were the pride of every good women's fashion journal, and while today fashion plates have been set aside for modern photography, the legacy of the fashion plate lingers; the term "fashion plate" now signifies a fashionable or trendy woman — while fashion plates of old are a collector's prize.

The Craze for Color...Yesterday

Though black and white plates were used from their inception right up to their demise, colored plates are what were most prized in days of old — and today. The first colored plates, which were usually about 8" high, were entirely hand colored by freelance watercolorists; most early magazines contained only a single colored plate, while featuring several more in black and white. By 1861, over sized plates that measured some 10 or more inches in length and were folded into the volume like a small map were not uncommon. Even standard-sized fashion plates increased in height to about 9½" to 10". While earlier plates had only sketchy backgrounds or no background at all and usually featured only one or two women in the latest styles, the new plates could feature five to seven women in full mode. Backgrounds were becoming more and more important and an "atmospheric" effect that placed women and their dresses at fashionable watering places and evening soirees became desirable.

Godey's Lady's Book, without a doubt the most popular American fashion magazine of the mid-nineteenth century, paid up to 150 women to color the some 100 color plates featured in a year's worth of the magazine. Many readers assumed the colors used in these watercolor plates were supposed to represent the latest fashionable shades; however, the truth was that though freelance colorists usually started with a color specified by the magazine's publisher, if they ran out of that color, they chose another shade at their own discretion. (When two readers wrote to the publisher of *Godey's* complaining that between the two of them, their fashion plates never matched, Mr. Godey diplomatically explained that a lady should not choose her colors by what was the fad of the day, but by what best suited her.)

Though fashion magazines produced in the United States often featured colored plates marked "Parisian," many so-called Paris plates were copied from German periodicals or from other American magazines. In fact, most of the magazines favored by Americans, including *Godey's Lady's Book, Young Ladies' Journal,* and *Peterson's Magazine,* copied fashion plates from European or other American journals, adjusting their illustrations only slightly.

By the 1880s, most fashion plates featured some hint of activity, whether of women dancing, sewing, or having tea. The 1890s saw the pinnacle of beauty in fashion plates, and many magazines produced by the sewing pattern industry, including *The Standard Designer* and *The Delineator,* produced fashion plates of rare and exemplary quality, using the widest variety of colors and the most carefully executed artistic touches, even though the plates were no longer colored by hand. This fine quality remained fairly consistent throughout the early 1900s and teens, until, in the 1920s, most fashion plates became distorted-looking and "arty." Such plates were often rendered by leading artists such as Erte and Barbier. In the 1930s, the distorted look persisted until, in the mid-30s, fashion plates slowly drowned in a sea of less expensive, less time-consuming fashion photographs and sketches.

...Today

For today's adept collector, fashion plates are fast becoming a favorite. For antique fashion collectors, in particular, fashion plates are a savvy collectible; the plates are a good way to date and identify existing period fashions (though it should be remembered that only the trendiest people wore fashions as exaggerated and flamboyant as most fashion plates depict). A good-sized collection, spanning over any particular epoch (such as the American Civil War or the 1890s, for example), is also extremely valuable, and in demand by scholars, museum curators, and collectors alike.

Most collectors won't be able to find plates from before the 1840s, but a vast number of fashion plates still exist from the late 1850s forward; the most readily available fashion plates come from the turn of the century. Collectors should be aware, however, that there are fakes in the fashion plate world. These fakes are actually reprints, made in eras much later than the fashions they depict. During the Victorian era, for example, many "costume plates" were printed of fashions from previous eras. However, knowing when fashion plates were first introduced will help you deduce that these plates are definitely not from the era they depict. Equally as common are Victorian-style plates that were printed in the 1920s through 1950s. Often a printer's logo can be found on the front or back of such plates — something that never appears on genuine historical fashion plates. (*Godey's Lady's Book* fashion plates are especially common; just remember that Godey's was published in America, not Italy!) Other times, however, collectors must rely on other clues to determine whether or not the plate is a fake. If, for example, the colors in a pre-1860s plate are brilliant, the plate is not authentic. And if the coloring does not show the variances of being handcolored (not precisely machine printed), it is probably not authentic. In the same vein, if any fashion plate is printed on glossy paper, it is unquestionably a reprint; most authentic plates were printed on heavy paper somewhat similar to today's construction paper.

One of the best indicators of a plate's authenticity is condition. If you run across fashion plates that are in mint condition, be skeptical.

Authentic plates, even though they might be in very good condition, have yellow "foxing" marks along the edges of the paper — a natural effect of aging. Collectors should also beware of plates that depict people in seemingly pre-Victorian dress or theatrical costumes. Such plates were featured alongside regular fashion plates in many Victorian fashion magazines, and depicted "fancy dress" or masquerade costumes. These are certainly collectible, but they are often found on the market dated to a much earlier time period than from which they originated. I advise novice fashion plate collectors to avoid fancy dress plates at first; as you develop your collection, you'll soon be able to identify what era such plates date from by noting the style of drawing used and the hairstyles and facial features of the models.

Fashion plates from nearly any magazine are considered collectible as long as they are in good condition. Some magazines printed rather crude renderings, especially those before the 1860s; these, naturally, are less desirable than more artistic plates. Many plates have already been removed from their original magazines, but this does not usually affect the value of the plate; however, if you can find the plates intact in the original magazine, so much the better. Fashion magazines are also historically significant and collectible, so if the plate isn't in any danger of being damaged, keeping it in its original magazine will only increase its value. Too, magazines complete with their color fashion plates are becoming more rare and therefore are valued more highly than magazines without their plates intact.

And while color plates are generally considered to be of more monetary value, black and white plates are equally as important to those interested in fashion history. Possibly the least desirable are fashion plates from the 1920s that are printed in one or two colors (often orange or green).

While still useful for reference, even crisp black and white fashion plates are more sought after than these. When choosing plates to add to your collection, it is always wise to avoid fashion plates with rips or tears, fading, or crinkling. If you purchase any plates that have been removed from magazines, try to buy only those that have been removed with a clean cut (not a rip).

Keeper of the Plates

One of the nicest things about fashion plates is that they're easy to put on display and can make stunning decoration. Framing is the usual route, but remember if they're not framed under ultraviolet reducing glass, they will fade. Even if you cannot afford special matting, a colored plate placed in a frame makes a pleasing display. I've even seen black and white plates framed beautifully (and inexpensively) by adhering them to black paper (using archival, easy to remove mounts available at framing shops) leaving a three-or four-inch margin around the edges of the plate, creating a mat. The edges of the plate are then trimmed with lace and the entire piece is framed. It is stunning and easily holds its own next to colored plates.

To keep unframed fashion plates in good condition, never use albums with sticky-backed pages, since eventually it will be next to impossible to remove the plates without tearing them. I recommend that you use an old-fashioned, plain-papered scrapbook with some archival-quality photo corners. Personally, I like to make a good color copy of the original fashion plate and place this in a loose-leaf notebook. The original can then be carefully stored in an acid-free scrapbook, while the copies serve as handy reference.

Offering an unprecedented glimpse of the fashions, artwork, and customs of the past, well cared for fashion plates are the demand of foresighted collectors and scholars, and as we approach the twenty-first century, they will continue to become more collectible and valuable.

An assortment of women's fashion magazines and plates, ranging in date from the 1820s to the 1880s.

Embroidered Fashion Plates

Within the past few years I have spotted an increasing number of unusual "fashion plates" popping up in antique stores. A beautiful combination of painting and needlework, these little gems began as needlework kits in the 1920s – 1930s but have risen into an artistic and savvy collectible, especially for antique fashion enthusiasts.

Each embroidered fashion plate is a copy of an authentic Victorian fashion plate from Godey's Lady's Book *dating to c.1840s – 1870s. Varying in size from about four inches to some 10 inches high, the date printed on the picture is often mistaken for the date of origin, but it is the date the authentic fashion plate appeared in* Godey's, *and not the date the picture was stitched.*

Fashion Plates & Reality

At a recent conference where a number of historical fashion enthusiasts gathered, I over-heard an interesting conversation between two women. One lady was twentyish, dark haired, and overflowing with bubbly enthusiasm for everything that had to do with Victorian women's fashions. The second lady was a redhead, perhaps 10 years older, a bit taller, and (while enjoy-ing herself) more quiet and reserved. I happened to be standing at a booth where these two women were chit-chatting, when, in the middle of their pleasant conversation, Quiet looked up, and suddenly seeing a woman costumed in 1890s dress walking across the room, pointed to her. Bubbly's eyes followed Quiet's gaze and a wide smile appeared on her face. "She looks darling, doesn't she?" said Bubbly to Quiet. "Yes," Quiet agreed. "But her costume's a bit off," Bubbly added. Quiet looked at Bubbly with a perplexed expression. Bubbly shrugged her shoulders. "It's just not quite right. If I held up a fashion plate from The Delineator *next to her, you'd see it immediately."*

Quiet and Bubbly looked again at the costumed lady as she conversed some distance away from them with other conference-goers. Said Quiet to Bubbly: "But compare her to a photograph from the period and she'd look just right."

As fashion collectors, we naturally admire and often collect the beautiful fashion plates from eras we most appreciate. We even use these fashion plates to help us date fashions, or to give us a better idea of just what the fashions of any given period looked like. But many of us forget one vital piece of information: fashion plates were not drawn from women on the streets; they were drawn from designers' and artists' imaginations.

For anyone who believes that fashion plates are an accurate representation of historical fash-ions, I urge them to begin collecting both fashion plates and photographs from the same era. The larger this collection grows, the more you'll realize how very different fashion plates are from period photographs. Even a brief look through this book, comparing the fashion plates and the period photographs included, should begin to give you an idea of the wide gulf between the two.

To fully appreciate this little study, remember that just like today (with the exception of snapshots), people wore their best clothes when they had their photographs taken; this phenom-enon was perhaps even more heightened during the Victorian period since the photos would be on open display in parlors where they were expected to impress visitors.

Even a cursory study will show great differences between what fashion plates claimed was being worn and what photographs reveal was actually worn. The photos show women's waists are generally wider and their skirts aren't held out by wide hoops. They may not wear the mandatory hat or gloves. They may not have the essential wasp-waist. (They may not even be wearing corsets!) They may have bulges high on their backs (the result of corsets), which fash-ion plates never picture. They may have rounded bellies (making them almost look pregnant) where fashion plates depict flat stomachs. They may have obvious bosoms where fashion plates show flat-chested flappers. Their hair may be in a simple bun where fashion plates show elabo-rate hairdos. The list goes on and on.

Now, I'm not suggesting you no longer collect fashion plates, or admire them, or even use them as a partial way to date existing historical fashions. I love fashion plates and use them as a general point of reference. But collectors and fashion enthusiasts should remember that just as few women look like the photographs given in a modern issue of Vogue *or* Mademoiselle, *few women of the past looked like fashion plates. Very few indeed. This is true of every era.*

The point is this: fashion plates are fiction, photographs are reality.

Women's fashion magazines of the early nineteenth century often featured hand-painted, elaborate title pages. *The Ladies' Magazine* later became *Peterson's Magazine.* Complete years' bound copy with color pages $50.00 – 150.00 each.

Newest Fashions for February 1829
Walking & Evening Dresses.

W. Alais Sc.

Color in early plates like these from the 1830s was faint compared to later fashion plates. $35.00 – 65.00.

Some of the most detailed fashion plates came from magazines that were published for the purpose of selling sewing patterns. This plate from the 1870s comes from *Butterick's Metropolitan.* $20.00 – 35.00.

An 1824 fashion plate. $30.00 – 70.00.

A fashion plate from the 1870s.
$15.00 – 30.00.

A fashion plate for *McCall's*
sewing patterns of the teens.
$15.00 – 30.00.

Black and white fashion plates can also be framed attractively;
a bit of lace trim perks them up. Unmounted, $1.00 – 5.00 ea.
Mounted, $10.00 – 25.00 ea.

An embroidered fashion plate taken from an 1845 original. It measures approximately 7" tall and 5" wide. $40.00 – 65.00.

An embroidered fashion plate based upon an 1848 *Godey's* original. Approximately 9" tall and 6" wide. $20.00 – 35.00.

A masterfully-executed embroidered fashion plate measuring approximately 6" wide and 8" tall, based on an 1870s *Godey's* fashion plate. $60.00 – 75.00.

The fantasy of fashion, from *Godey's Lady's Book.*

The reality of fashion.

Part Two

The Collecting

Chapter Thirteen
Shaping & Building A Collection

By now, you're probably chomping at the bit to go out and hoard some collectible fashions — that is, if you've managed to contain yourself up until now! If you're just starting out as a fashion collector, however, you may wonder where's the best place to begin? There are auctions, antique shops, vintage clothing shops, flea markets, mail order dealers — where does a poor soul dare to begin?

Two good first steps for most beginning collectors are to discover what fashions from which eras they prefer and to get familiar with the real thing. A great way to do this is look up books at your local library under headings such as "Costume," and "Fashion, Historic." Your library should have at least one or two books with pictures of fashion throughout history; from these, you can decide which eras most interest you. If you enjoy the high-tech way of doing things, check out fashion sites on the Internet; many museums (including the biggies like the Metropolitan Museum of Art) have websites, and there are a growing number of web sites specifically for antique and vintage fashion collectors.

Complete your entry-level education by going to museum exhibits and historic fashion shows or shops. There is nothing like seeing the real thing up close and personal; details are important and can keep you from purchasing what you believe to be an authentic, high-waisted c.1800 gown only later to discover you were mistaken and it actually dates to the 1890s. Notice fabrics — the designs on them, their look, and (if you're not at a museum) their feel and weight.

Learn what kind of closures are common during various eras and what the inside of period garments look like. You'll begin to get a feel for which eras most fascinate you and which eras you'd most like to collect. It's also a great idea to begin acquiring a library of books, both period and modern, that depict historic fashions.

With this information in hand, you can collect with some certainty. If, however, you run across an item that you're uncertain about at an antique shop, never hesitate to ask the dealer about it. Sometimes dealers don't know any more than you do, but they may be able to help shed some light on the matter. Few dealers will accept returns, so even if you (or the dealer) makes a mistake in regards to identification, you'll have to live with it. So shop carefully. If you love something and think the price is fair, it's hard to lose.

Decisions, Decisions
Some collectors are very meticulous about what they buy, especially if they've been collecting for some time. It's true that narrowing your collection does tend to make the hunt a little more challenging (and for many, that's half the fun!). Too, many people prefer to have a spectacular collection of all hats from the 1940s, or all beaded bags from the 1920s, or only party dresses from the 1950s. Other possibilities for specialized fashion collections include collecting by type of garment (i.e., evening gowns, frock suits, lingerie), by designer, or by material (i.e., beaded fabrics, furs). Another possibility that is ideal for beginners is to shape a col-

lection by wardrobe. Think of this as shaping a trousseau; you may begin with a skirt and blouse, then move on to an evening dress, a few hats, etc.

The most popular approach to collecting, however, is undoubtedly "a little here, a little there." This method is tried and true (and rarely dull!), and leads to a multi-faceted collection. I tend to collect in this manner, and have garments ranging from the 1840s through the 1960s, including clothes worn by royalty, prairie dresses, designer fashions, and home-made clothes.

But just how do you go about building your collection? The following chapters will give you some specifics, but in general, the first thing you'll want to do is go to local vintage clothing shops and assess the period, style, and quality of the materials each dealer carries. Get aquatinted with your local dealers. Let them know where your interests lie; if you're specific enough about this, dealers may begin to purchase items they think you'd be interested in. Also become familiar with what local auctions, flea markets, and estate sales tend to carry in the area of collectible fashions.

Let everyone (your family, friends, fellow employees, schoolmates, etc.) know you're interested in collectible clothing. Be sure to tell them you're willing to buy items from them; also tell them what eras or styles you're interested in, since otherwise they're likely to assume you only want either very old clothing, or more modern ("retro") clothing.

After a while, you may wish to advertise. In most periodicals that focus on historical fashions, there are classified advertisements available for readers to make their wants known. Even more general antique and collectible periodicals are good places to put advertisements. You might even consider posting your interest on an Internet bulletin board. Be as specific as possible in these ads, and once they appear, you're likely to be swamped with offers.

With all these sources for vintage fashions, you might be tempted to buy much more than you want or need. (We all go through periods where we feel like we'd like to hoard every flapper beaded dress, or turn-of-the-century lingerie dress, or 1950s evening gown.) Antique and vin-tage fashion collectors are especially notorious for buying things they don't especially like or that are less worthwhile because they are in such terrible condition or because some modern collector has badly repaired them (iron-on patching tape is the thorn in the side of every collector!); we use excuses like "it's such a good deal," or "the poor thing, it needs a good home." My best advice to you is to try to fight such temptations. If you don't love it, why buy it? Why spend $50.00 on a 1930s dress that you don't especially like, when you could spend that money on something you really love?

The Art Of Buying At Auctions

Collectors attend auctions to find items they can't find elsewhere. They explore auctions hoping to discover the buy of the century. They go to auctions for the sheer excitement of them.

But a collector who does not know and understand the maxims of auction-going may instead discover disaster. Bidding more than you can afford to pay, buying items you didn't really want, ending up with items you didn't realize were in poor condition — these are all consequences of poor auction-going. It needn't be this way, of course; auctions can easily be fun and successful.

Choosing An Auction

The first step to effective auction-going is choosing an auction that suits your needs. In your initial search, scan publications covering collectible fashions and antiques and look through the classified listings in local newspapers. Most auction advertisements list items to be sold, but if they do not, or if you want a more complete understanding of what will be up for bid, call the phone number given in the ad for details.

Next, determine how "rich" the auction will be. Every collector probably knows that a Sotheby's or Christie's auction is generally for very serious, affluent collectors, but there are also many local auction houses that cater to the well-to-do. Hints that an auction may be beyond the average collector's means include words like "finest," "exquisite," and "premium," in their advertisements. Another important considera-tion is whether or not the auction is a "country" auction. Generally, country (sometimes called "estate") auctions are sources of the best buys; however, prices realized at any auction are usually related to the crowd size; a smaller crowd usually brings the lowest prices.

Before blissfully running off to an auction, it's a good idea to assess your needs. What additions to your collection would you like to make? If, for instance, you have a collection of flapper costumes, do you want to add a beaded dress to your collection? And do you already have a number of hats and don't want any more for the time being? Perhaps you have a large quantity of black items in your collection; do you want to veer away from black and stick to color for the time being? Write down your needs and unnecessaries and bring the list with your to the preview and auction, as a gentle reminder.

Do you have a limit of how much money you can spend? (Most of us do, unfortunately!) Figure out a budget, write it down, and take it with you to the preview and auction — as a firm reminder when you're tempted to indulge when you really shouldn't.

Previews

If you want to buy at any auction, it is important to attend the auction's preview. It's then that you will be allowed to examine all items to be auctioned, making certain they are in acceptable condition and indeed what you want and/or need. If the advertisement for the auction did not list a preview time, call the auction house for information. Be wary of auction houses that do not offer previews.

Once at the preview, carefully examine anything you are considering bidding on. Check for any faults: loose or missing buttons or trims, tears, holes, shattered fabrics, etc. Remember that once the auctioneer cries "Sold!," the item is yours.

After carefully examining the items you intend to bid on, figure the highest amount you are willing to pay for each; write this number down (along with the lot or box number, if there is one) and stick to it. Remember that any applicable sales tax must be added onto your purchase price, in addition to any buyer's premium the auction house may have (ten percent is the usual).

At The Auction

You may be at the auction all day, so for your own comfort, come prepared. Don't count on the auction house providing food or drink; bring your own chair and a comfortable cushion, too.

Come early to the auction to reinspect all items you want to bid on. Sometimes items get put into different lots or boxes than they were at the preview — either by accident or by unscrupulous bidders. There's also the possibility the item may have been damaged by rough handling since the preview.

Your final preparation for the auction will be to obtain a bidding card or paddle from the auctioneer. To do so, you usually must provide I.D. and show an ability to pay — normally by cash or check; credit cards are not usually accepted.

Does it matter where you sit at an auction? Absolutely! If you get to the auction at least an hour early, you should be able to get a front seat. Here, you can easily see the items up for bid and the auctioneer can easily hear you or see your bidding card. Often at the beginning of an auction people are hesitant to bid — and toward the end of an auction, many people are tired and not alert, having purchased the items they wanted, and are off paying the auctioneer. Therefore, good buys can often be had at these times and your front row seating will ensure that you aren't distracted by a throng of weary auction-goers.

Bidding

Don't worry, the flick of a finger or the nod of a head won't be considered a bid. Only the clear raising of a bidding card or paddle above the head (sometimes with an audible cry of the amount bidding) will be considered a valid bid by the auctioneer. Don't be timid; when you're ready to bid, go ahead and bid before someone else beats you to the punch.

If there are many similar items to be auctioned off, you may wish to wait for the last ones; the price usually drops on these last items because the desire for them is often nearly satisfied. Sometimes if there are several similar items available, the auctioneer may offer "bidder's choice." This means the highest bidder get first choice among the items, the second highest bidder gets second choice, etc.

It's all too easy to get caught up in the excitement of a bidding war — but it's best to stop bidding once the price rises higher than the price you have written down and promised yourself to pay. This will save you the rent — and hindsight regret for over-paying.

Above all, enjoy yourself. Auctions are rewarding and entertaining; planning and buying shrewdness should never interfere with happy hunting.

Shopping Through The Mail

If you are looking to expand and round-off your collection of vintage fashions, mail order will probably be your most valued source. Unlike most local stores, which can't carry very fine or rare items (because they wouldn't be able to sell them as quickly as their overhead requires them to), mail order dealers can carry a wider variety of items, including fine and rare garments, designer clothes, and foreign fashions.

How it Works

Many collectors wonder how on earth you can buy vintage clothes by mail, but it's usually a simple and pleasant experience. You can find mail order sources by browsing through a couple of magazines that cover collectible fashions; contact each dealer as they request you do in their advertisement. This often means writing down your specific wants (including type of garment, condition desired, and price range) and sending off a self-addressed, stamped envelope. Sometimes you'll need to send money for a price list or catalog. (You've probably heard it before, but it bears repeating: Never send cash; always send a check — because you never know when something might get lost in the mail.)

In return, each dealer will send you a description of the items they are selling, along with their condition, price, and (preferably but not always) a photograph or sketch. This information may come in a variety of ways. Some dealers have full color catalogs or catalogs with black and white illustrations; others have catalogs with no pictures whatsoever, just descriptions and prices; while still others offer video tapes. Some dealers will even write you person-

alized letters with information on the stock that might interest you.

All dealers should also send you some kind of information on their terms. Sometimes this is an actual contract that you must sign, but most often it's just a sheet detailing the company's mail order policies. The most important thing to look for is the promise that the dealer will offer you a full refund (though it will usually be minus shipping costs) if you aren't completely satisfied with your order. This is particularly important when buying collectible fashions through the mail, since your concept of any particular item's condition may vary from the dealer's.

Be wary of dealers who don't give you phone numbers with their catalog or ordering information. Most dealers actually want you to call them in order to reserve items you wish to buy; otherwise, you might order something only to find out it has already been sold to another customer.

When filling out your order, remember that shipping is almost always added to your overall cost. Sometimes specific shipping charges are given in the dealer's catalog, but if they are not, it's a good idea to call the dealer and get a ball-park figure. Sales tax (where applicable) also must be added if the dealer has an office or shop in your state.

The Internet

There is also an electronic twist to shopping via mail: the Internet. Here, you can meet up with other fashion collectors through bulletin boards and swap or buy garments from around the world. Too, there's a growing number of antique dealer sites to choose from — and some specialize in fashions. Your best bet is not to look for cites geared toward general antiques but to seek out sites specifically on historical fashions. Here, photos are posted along with prices and descriptions; you never know what kind of treasure you might find and have shipped right to your doorstep!

But whether you buy from traditional catalogs or from Internet sites, mail order is a hassle-free way to expand your collection and supplement your local vintage fashion scene.

When's a Bargain a Bargain?

The issue of bargaining is a sensitive one. Generally, at shows where a large number of dealers are gathered for a few days, bargaining is expected. And while the majority of antique dealers in shops also anticipate a bit of bargaining, some shop dealers find it insulting.

If you've looked carefully over a piece and have some legitimate reasons why you would like to see the price lowered, by all means, approach the dealer. Generally, the accepted way to do this is to say something like, "Would you consider taking X amount of dollars for this piece?" or "Is your price firm?" If the dealer who owns the piece is not present in the shop, ask if you can leave a note with your name, number, and offer. If you know the piece is mis-dated, politely and diplomatically point this out: "This dress is marked Civil War era, but the raised waistline and slim skirt indicate that it's from the teens." Some dealers won't pay much attention to this, but a good fashion dealer will at least listen, smile, and give you her reasoning for the date and price on the piece.

Sometimes you'll run across price tags marked "as is." This means the dealer recognizes that there are flaws on the garment but is firm on the price. But if a price tag is absent of this mark, collectors should feel free to bargain using legitimate flaws as points of reference. For example, if a certain girl's dress from the 1890s is marked $75.00, but you can see upon close examination that the red silk of the collar, yolk, and cuffs is beginning to shatter, point this out to the dealer. She may agree to lower the price accordingly.

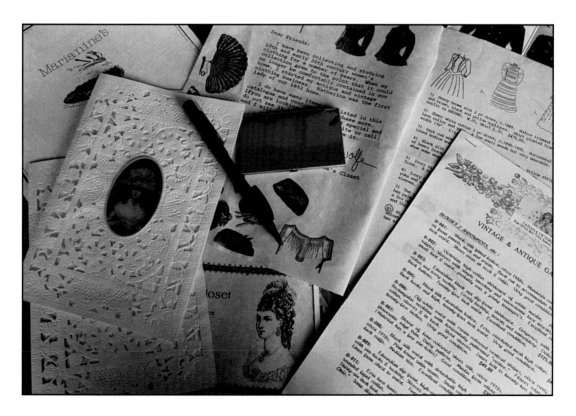

There are a wide variety of mail order sources, for a variety of budgets.

Chapter Fourteen
Care & Display

The prospect of proper storage and care can seem to be the impossible dream. Many collectors, after reading manuals geared toward museum curators, shake their heads and simply come to the conclusion, "I am not a museum." This is true, of course, but collectors also have a responsiblity to take care of the historical fashions in their homes. When it comes right down to it, proper care of collectible fashions means the difference between a collection that increases in value over the years and a collection that de-values over the years.

It's also important to remember that there were only so many historical clothes ever created; most are long since destroyed. The few that remain, then, need to be cherished and well-cared for if we want future generations to be able to appreciate, learn from, and enjoy them.

Natural fabrics (which is all there were until rayon was introduced in the 1920s) begin to decay the moment they are picked or cut. Man-made fabrics have their own special problems, tending to be weaker than natural fabrics and therefore generally more likely to fall apart. But fabric decay of any kind can be sped up or slowed down. Things that increase the rate of fabric deterioration include direct light, perspiration, dust and dirt, stains, insects, dry air, and damp air.

To Clean or Not to Clean

The first thing to do in caring for your collection is make sure pests don't invade the pieces. Whenever you adopt any old textiles or paper goods, shake them off outside; if any dead bugs fly off or if you spy any eggs or larvae, stick the offending item in a plastic bag, seal it thoroughly with duct tape, and put it in the freezer for a few days — that'll kill the critters!

The next consideration is keeping your garments relatively clean — but just how to clean antique and vintage clothing is a big problem for collectors. Ideally, all collectors should take their historical clothing to a professional conservator for care and cleaning; however, this is impossible for most collectors, so here are some basic rules of thumb to follow:

1. Ask your dealer (or the previous owner of the garment) if it has been cleaned already; if it has, don't wash it again! Every time you wash a garment, its fabric becomes a little weaker.

2. If the garment is very delicate or old, vacuum it. Place a piece of screening or dense netting (the edges covered with tape) over the garment and use a handheld vac to pick up soil from the surface of the fabric. If a screen is not available, cover the vac head with cheesecloth and hold the vac several inches away from the garment as you clean. Be careful not to suck the garment's fabric into the vac. If the garment is still musty-smelling, air it by placing it in a room (on a sweater rack or on a bed) with all the windows open. Be sure the garment is not in direct sunlight, which is damaging to fabric.

3. Garments that aren't washable (like those of wool or silk, or garments with linings) and need more cleaning than vacuuming can provide can be taken to a dry cleaner. Try to find a cleaner that a local museum trusts or one that specializes in delicate or bridal fabrics. Ask the cleaner to put the garment in a mesh bag and clean the garment only after the old cleaning solvent has been replaced. In lieu of a mesh cleaning bag, you can prepare the garment for the cleaner by sandwiching it between two layers of muslin and basting the layers together along the outline of the garment; before you do this, however, be sure to remove any buttons or other trims that might not take well to dry cleaning. In any case, you should be fully aware that dry cleaning can sometimes do more harm than good. If the garment is made of silk, for instance, and is brittle to

the touch, dry cleaning may only make the fabric more brittle and fragile. One dealer has even told me that when she recently took a designer gown to the dry cleaner, it came back in shreds. In less extreme cases, dry cleaning will do absolutely nothing to clean a garment, and in fact, will sometimes cause more dirt to be held into the garment's fibers. White garments will also sometimes turn yellow when dry cleaned.

4. Use a large sink or the bathtub when cleaning washable vintage clothing, placing a piece of muslin or a white cotton sheet on the bottom. Fill the basin with lukewarm water; if your water has a high chemical content, use only ionized or bottled water. Add your cleaning agent — very little will be needed for one garment; read the bottled instructions on Orvus (most easily found in fabric shops under the product name "Quilt Care") for specific measurements, or use about ⅛ of a 3½ oz. bar of Neutrogena face wash soap mixed with a cup of water, and add this to every gallon of washing water. Now add the garment, making sure it gets thoroughly wet. Agitate the garment gently with your hands. The garment may then soak for up to a half hour — but no longer, unless fresh soaking water is exchanged for the old. Drain the water, holding the garment up from the drain by picking up the edges of the muslin. Gently rinse the garment, pressing out the soap, not squeezing or twisting. Be sure to rinse out all the soap; the less soap you use, the easier it will be to rinse out.

5. If white garments still appear yellow after washing, use "Sodium Perborate" bleach only (a product available through archival product companies), but remember that many old white clothes were actually off-white in color.

6. Dry washed garments flat on a sweater rack or on a thick white towel. You can dry the garment outside on days that aren't damp, but it is best not to allow the garment to sit in direct sunlight. Also be careful not to place the garment in areas where it may be easily stained by grass, animals, etc. In areas where air pollution is high, do not dry garments out of doors.

To Display or Not to Display

The next difficulty comes when you try to decide what to do with all those old clothes in your collection. People who collect old pottery or furniture or books can readily display their collections. Can vintage fashion collectors do the same without risking the ruin their collection? Yes! In fact, a growing number of collectors are not only displaying pieces of their collection in their homes but are lending items for local museum and historic building displays — a great way to pass on and share a love for "old clothes!" Accomplishing a safe and effective way to display a personal collection (whether at home or in a public setting) can be time consuming; there are many factors to consider, but the results can be rewarding.

Light

Museums prefer that the rooms where costumes are displayed have no windows and no vents for daylight — but this isn't very practical for personal collectors. Instead, choose areas where direct daylight doesn't hit.

Because textiles are especially prone to light damage, any showcases used should be the kind treated with ultraviolet protectors. Any showcase lights should be as weak as possible, adding just enough light to enhance the item on display. Your choice of backdrop color may affect the lighting needed, also; a lighter color background generally needs less light than a darker one.

Dirt and Humidity

Because dirt is a great hindrance to textiles, the room where your costumes are displayed should be as dust free as possible. You might even consider purchasing an ionizer (a machine that actually cleans and filters the air); not only will this help keep your displayed treasures cleaner, it may actually improve your health — especially if you suffer from allergies.

In fighting the war against dust, however, do not buy completely encasing display cases. Your textiles need ventilation to protect them from humidity — which is a great destroyer of textiles and will cause mold and mildew.

Mountings

The most difficult part of putting together a display is figuring out how to mount the costumes. Museums battle with this problem daily. What method best suits the costumes? What method is least harmful to the costumes?

Which methods are within our budget? Which lend themselves to our allotted space? If even the country's best museums express difficulties with mounting fashions, how on earth can collectors hope to conquer the problem?

First, accept the fact that you are not a museum. Nobody expects your display, public or otherwise, to be as intricate and involved as a display at the Metropolitan Museum of Art. (And I doubt you want your home to look like a museum, anyway.)

Then, consider what you have on hand. If you're setting up a display for a public place, perhaps they have their own methods and materials that you can use. If not, perhaps they'll be interested in acquiring some for use in ongoing exhibits.

Otherwise, you'll need to think creatively. Do you have any mannequins on hand? If you're working on a public display, perhaps you can borrow some from a local college or vintage clothing store. Either dressmaker forms or storefront mannequins will work. (However, if you decide upon the latter, they will preferably be those that are true to the period of clothing you are presenting, since a modern, slouching, wide-waisted mannequin will tend to make all but modern clothes look frumpy.) If dressmaker forms or full-bodied mannequins are not available, consider creating your own dressmaker forms by one of the many methods sewing magazines frequently tout. You can even create stuffed torsos (which can be hung from the ceiling by fishing line) that will give the basic impression of a human form under the clothes.

While the three-dimensional look of a mannequin is always preferred, there are other possibilities. Perhaps you can lay the garments flat in a shallow display case (this is ideal for many accessories). Larger garments can be suspended from fabric tapes that can then be pinned onto a wall.

Some other general points to remember when displaying your collection:

• Always display garments with appropriate undergarments, including hoops, bustles, and petticoats. Petticoats and hoops can be simulated by taping heavy kraft paper onto the mannequin in the desired width and shape. (The resulting foundation should then be covered with unbleached muslin in order to protect the garment being displayed from the harmful acids of the paper.) Bustles can also be simulated by stuffing a pillowcase into an appropriate shape, then tying it around the waist of the mannequin. Not only do such foundations give the correct period shape, but they also help support and lessen the strain on garments so that the chances of tears or other wearing while they are on display are greatly reduced.

• Pins are sometimes found in garments as originally used. It is best to remove these and repair tears, fastenings, etc. Decorative or fashion pins, such as brooches or skirt elevators, can certainly be used in garment displays, but should always be checked for deterioration (such as rust) before being placed on the costume (and should always be removed before storing the costume).

• Unless a garment is already in very poor condition, care should be taken that it is not kept on display for long periods of time. Even a few weeks of sitting on a mannequin can cause great strain on some old fabrics. This is why many collectors only display poor condition garments, framed small pieces, and accessories in display cases in their home.

Washing Rayon

Recently I acquired a box of rayon dresses from the 1930s – 1940s. They were all in wonderful condition, but I bought them for a song. How'd I manage it? Easy. After decades of sitting in their original owner's damp garage, the dresses had assumed an alarming stench. But being the true vintage clothing trouper that I am, I snatched them up, thinking it'd be easy to get them fresh-smelling once again.

Hmmmm...if only it had been that simple.

First, I considered dry cleaning the dresses, but I was afraid they'd end up brittle, so I decided that a good steaming would do the trick. With my trusty hand-held steamer, I steamed and steamed the dresses in a well-ventilated area of the house. The fabric seemed rejuvenated by the eye, and certainly I managed to get all the wrinkles out, but rather than removing the foul smell, I just managed to make my eyes water.

I was aghast. The dresses were terrific, but nobody — not even the most stout-hearted vintage clothing enthusiast — could endure their musty smell. With a painful gulp, I realized I'd have to wash the dresses.

Now normally, I enjoy a good washing session — but when it comes to rayon...let's just say that I recommend avoiding it whenever possible. Sometimes it's inevitable, however, so here's the low-down on the easiest method I've discovered.

The first trick is to use neither hot nor cold water — lukewarm or cool is best. Always use the gentlest soap you can find; a very small amount of Neutrogena does the job nicely. Often the garment will begin to lose dye as soon as it hits the water — don't panic! This is perfectly normal since many old rayons have never been washed. Still, it's wise to wash only one garment at a time, so that the different colored dyes don't intermingle. I should also point out here that some rayons cannot be washed — especially those from the 1920s — because they will shrink dramatically. So if you have rayons from before the 1940s, don't wash them unless the garment is valueless otherwise. If there is any question on this point, test a small, inconspicuous spot.

Rayon will withstand very little agitation — the man-made fabric tends to become extremely weak and will lose its shape if twisted or stretched while wet. Therefore, agitate by pressing the garment. Once the garment seems clean, drain the sink, holding the fabric away from the drainpipe. With a little cool (not cold) water running over the garment, press out all soap bubbles.

Next, lay the garment flat on top of a thick towel (some dye may stain the towel, so make sure it's not from your best set) and rest it on a counter or floor. Allow the garment to dry away from direct sunlight. To reduce the number of wrinkles in the garment, gently unfold major wrinkles immediately.

Finally, while the fabric is still damp, press it with a cool iron on the wrong side of the garment until dry. If you must press details from the right side of the garment, use a good pressing cloth to prevent the iron from marring the fabric with a permanent shine.

15 Tips For Displays

Hats look terrific:
- *Sitting on hat stands on vanity tables*
- *Hung in a hallway or on a single wall, just as family photos traditionally do*
- *Hung on entryway coat racks, along with parasols or vintage umbrellas in accompanying umbrella stands*
- *Hung on dressing room screens*
- *Hung on a bedpost*

Gloves are perfect:
- *As accessories for vanity tables*
- *Hung in groups on walls*

Drawers, stockings, and petticoats look great:
- *Hung on towel racks and washstands*

Fashion plates, photos, and patterns may be:
- *Tucked into the rims of mirrors*

Shoes can be:
- *Displayed on end-of-bed trunks*
- *Used even singly; a lone shoe with no mate can make a charming "vase" for dried flowers — or can be stuffed with fabric & hatpins stuck in it*

Bags are ideal:
- *Hung on pegs, drawer pulls, screens, doorknobs, and bed posts*

Handkerchiefs can be made into:
- *Table runners by tacking them together, corner to corner*

But in all cases:
- *Don't display anything in any of the above ways unless you are comfortable with the fact that they will probably be damaged and lose value*
- *Remember that good-condition pieces should be stored most of the time and displayed only with great care*

Garments artfully waiting to be used in a lecture when only one mannequin was available.

Purses can be hung from doorknobs — especially those that are rarely used, such as on a curio or china cabinet. $100.00 – 160.00.

Hats can easily be hung on the wall.

A single shoe can be an interesting addition to a bedroom; "dress it" with dried flowers, or use it in lieu of a hatpin holder.

Chapter Fifteen

The Truth About Provenance

It might seem as though purchasing a piece of vintage clothing considered "of special historical significance" is a rare (though thrilling) experience few private collectors have the good fortune to experience — unless they can afford to buy through Christie's or Sotheby's. But the truth is, at least once in their collecting career, almost every collector will run across an item to which some history behind the piece is known — a piece that has "provenance."

"There are really two levels of provenance," antiques expert Ed Hild says. "One is when a piece has been in someone's private collection." (For instance, if you acquired an Art Nouveau beaded bag that was once part of Barbra Sreisand's personal collection.) "True provenance," Ed notes, "where the history can be traced before the dealer had the object is very rare. It's often verbal and impossible to prove."

Most often, the history behind clothing is passed down by word of mouth. For instance, a few years ago, I acquired a slat bonnet and cape worn by a widow on the Oregon Trail. The woman who sold me the matching pair told me the story of the garments from memory. Unfortunately, while oral histories are fascinating, they mean little to circumspect historians (or, for that matter, your insurance agent) and are not considered to have actual, provable provenance.

Nonetheless, many collectors are in a wonderful position to obtain provenance. If, for example, you are fortunate enough to acquire a garment from the original owner, be certain to have them write down the piece's history and then sign and date it. This was the way a West Coast community theatre with an extensive antique clothing collection documented a particular top hat that was donated to them. A brief, typed paper related that the hat was worn at the signing of the Treaty of Versailles (near the

end of WWI) by Solicitor General of the United States, Fred Neilson. This account was verified by Mr. Neilson's widow's signature and a donation date. A written note by an ancestor of the original owner (like a spouse or child) is almost as good as obtaining a note from the original owner.

Sometimes such histories can be even more telling than they first appear. This was the case when dealer Joanne Haug acquired a baby bib from Florida's Lowe Art Museum. A note was attached to the bib, detailing who had donated the bib to the museum in the 1950s; then, a list of family members who wore the bib was included. Armed with this information, Joanne used the library to research the family's tree. Her findings? While the bib dated to the 1700s, the family tree led all the way back to the Mayflower!

The best kind of provenance is documentation that is so detailed it would be difficult for anyone to question it. (It is not coincidence that the word is spelled P-R-O-V-E-N-ance!) This includes photographs of the original owner wearing the garment, or perhaps letters describing the outfit, or even original bills of sale.

Of course, contrary to what some may imply, provenance doesn't actually increase the importance of a piece. (An authentic corset from the 16th century, for example, may certainly be "more important" to collectors and historians than a dress that originally belonged to Queen Marie Antoinette.) While even excellent provenance will not make an otherwise ill-made or unappealing item worth more money to collectors or historians, provenance does, nonetheless, often increase the monetary value of appealing items — sometimes are much as 50% depending upon how notable the person is you can trace it to — solely because it adds a certain sentimental aspect or fascination to the piece. Many collectors feel that only provenance gives a clear, human face to history. In the world of collectibles clothing, this sentiment is particularly strong.

So do yourself and everyone interested in historical fashions a favor. Memories are often inaccurate and oral histories usually become embellished before they are eventually forgotten. Write down everything you know about the history of all garments in your collection. Add strength to your documentation by adding photographs of the original owner (and if you can uncover photographs of the original owner wearing the garment, all the better!). If you can't get your hands on original photographs, make color copies of them. Add to this documentation any newspaper clippings or other paperwork that might be pertinent. And original authentic bills of sale for the item are always worth having. Case in point: when Joanne Haug purchased a pair of slippers from the 1860s, she was certain to hang onto a 1930s auction catalog and bill of sale that verified the shoes originally belonged to Queen Alexandria — not only adding historical interest to the slippers, but also increasing their monetary value considerably.

Be certain also to include the history of how you acquired the piece, from what person in what city, and for how much. Also keep your own receipt of sale and any information you can uncover about how the person who sold you the garment came to own it.

Keeping careful records of the history of antique and vintage fashions not only adds monetary value to your collection, more importantly, it adds a great deal of historical interest and significance. If the item in question was worn by your grandmother, write this information down (even if she didn't happen to be famous or involved in important historical activities). And if it survived a notable flood or earthquake, also write this down. And consider this: imagine for a moment that you find in one vintage clothing shop two identical, turn-of-the-century, beautiful white lace evening gowns. You love the design and want to take one gown home, but which one would you choose? The one without any provenance, or the one that comes with a hand-written, signed, and dated note from the original owner saying it survived the 1906 San Francisco earthquake?

Don't let the personality behind your collection become lost to history.

The Princess and the Capelet: The Provenance Behind One Very Special Garment

A few years ago, I attended a local antique show — not expecting to discover anything remarkable, just hoping to enjoy a brief romp through history. But as I neared the end of the numerous dealer stands, I paused at a display case featuring a lovely Edwardian capelet. The dealer eagerly let me examine the capelet up close and from her suddenly sprang a grand story — entirely documented with photos, newspaper clippings, and foreign passports.

Realizing the gem I was holding, I snatched up the capelet — and all the documentation — quickly. What had unfolded was a romantic, fairy-tale-like story that linked this beautiful capelet to a remarkable young Edwardian woman.

Once Upon A Time...

She was christened Princess Augusta Victoria Beatrice Bruckner Von Gotha of the House of Saxe-Coburg-Botha, but her friends called her Trudy — a nickname derived from her chosen name, Gertrude. This petite and pretty princess was born in 1885 in the Castle Liebenstein in the Thuringen region of Germany.

The Princess would later describe her castle as having some 300 rooms, seven kitchens, and 13 cooks; she had never counted how many servants were positioned in and outside the castle. As a princess, and as the offspring of one of Europe's wealthiest families, she was not educated in the usual manner. Most of her schooling centered on the arts, but she was also required to travel extensively and learned to speak several languages fluently.

Later in her life, the Princess laughed as she recalled how her grandmother required her to take her studies into the kitchen. "We were taught to 'cook'," the Princess said. "We'd watch someone peel a potato or prepare a simple dish. Then we'd write down the recipe and take notes. Actually, we never touched the food being prepared." The Princess protested every moment of these lessons, but her grandmother insisted that she and her sisters learn cookery. "Servants can quit...anything can happen to you — you never know," her grandmother said, eerily foretelling the Princess's future. "Some day you might need to be able to cook."

Even so, the Princess was required — and permitted — to do little. She was forbidden to associate with non-royalty, to the extent that even when she went ice skating, guards followed her, clearing a patch of ice exclusively for her use — apart from the commoners.

One of the more dramatic events of the Princess's youth, however, involved Czar Nicholas of Russia. At a banquet she attended with the Czar, his family, and other royalty, the cook served poisonous mushrooms. Fortunately, the Princess nor the Czar and his family partook of them — but at least one other princess died, Elizabeth Hesse-Darmstadt, niece of Queen Marie of Rumania. "One could only guess what happened to that particular cook," Princess Trudy later remarked.

As the Princess came of age, the pressures of her bloodline began to make themselves known. Her brothers and sisters all married royalty — as was the tradition. It had been presumed since the Princess's birth that she'd marry Count Erik Von Ludendorff, later a famous field marshal.

But in 1903, the Princess shocked the royal world...wearing the capelet I recently acquired, no less.

The Evening And the Capelet

The evening began much like many evenings in the Princess's life. There was a grand ball: fairy-tale-like, with royal men in uniforms and their ladies in the finest French gowns decorated with pearls and ermine. However, unlike other evenings, a young American man wearing a plain business suit slipped past the guards. The Princess and the American spotted each other. By all accounts, it was love at first sight.

When the Princess declared she would marry no one but the American, her parents were first shocked, then disappointed. Still, they allowed the Princess to do as she willed — but according to custom, she was forced to give up both her right to the family estate and her title.

"My great desire was for freedom," the Princess later declared, "the freedom only America can give. Always during my girlhood I was watched — every step, every move, every glance. I never could be alone, do as I liked, live as I wished." She quickly learned to love her new-found freedom, and felt overwhelmingly blessed by it many times in her life — especially when her family was thrown into a concentration camp for opposing Hitler's tyranny.

Her New Life

For several years, the Princess and her husband lived in Princeton, where it took her many years to adjust to her new way of life. For some time, the Princess said, her American neighbors thought her eccentric because she daily walked to her husband's hardware store dressed in one of her trained, velvet French gowns, lace and ribbon parasol clasped in hands protected by long, fine gloves. The Princess may have been able to clear up many of her neighbors' misgivings by acknowledging her heritage; however, her husband asked her not to, because he feared it would be bad for his business.

The rest of the Princess's life was largely reclusive. Her father died, then her only child, and then her cherished husband. Now living in the community of Redmond, Oregon, she remarried and continued to live a predominantly isolated life.

The Fate Of the Capelet

Shortly after the Princess's burial in 1966 (at which time the American world was finally allowed to know of her royal lineage), her second husband took ill and began living with a local Redmond family. Before he died, he gave many of the Princess's belongings away — mostly to friends. The daughter of the friend he was living with was fortunate enough to acquire several pieces of the Princess's jewelry, some of her documents, and the capelet she wore the evening she met her first husband. This woman was the dealer I met at a local antique show.

This man's Victorian hat is complete with its original box, which features not only the maker's name and address but also the owner's (in faint pencil): "Julius H. Caplan, 842 Walnut St., Lebanon, PA." $85.00 – 150.00.

Courtesy of Titiana Victoriana; photo by M. Eden Banik.

Photo courtesy of the Lassiter/Cheetham collection.

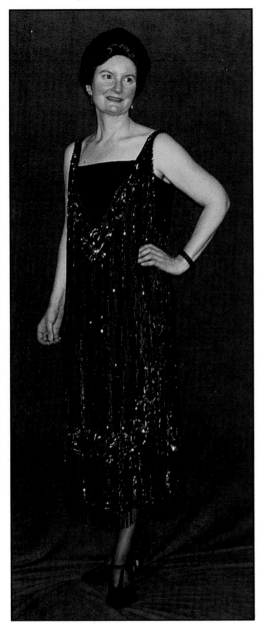

The history of this c.1892 – 1894 two-piece dress is known because it was purchased at an estate sale in Ohio; the name of the family member who wore the piece and related history were recorded by the dealer who acquired the dress, then later passed down to the collector who now owns it. $125.00 – 275.00.

Photo courtesy of the Lassiter/Cheetham collection.

An evening gown from c.1922 – 23; it was inherited from a wealthy relative who lived in Philadelphia and made seasonal trips to New York City to acquire the latest in fashion. Black, gold, and silver sequins completely cover the dress, and the skirt is fringed with tiny black beads. The matching silk charmeuse slip forms a modesty panel at the neckline. $175.00 – 295.00.

This 1856 day dress of changeable silk taffeta was originally worn by Elizabeth Ann Williams of Roxbury, Massachusetts. $400.00 – 800.00.

Photo courtesy of Karen Augusta.

Courtesy of the personal collection on Pam Coghlan.

Photo courtesy of the Lassiter/Cheetham collection.

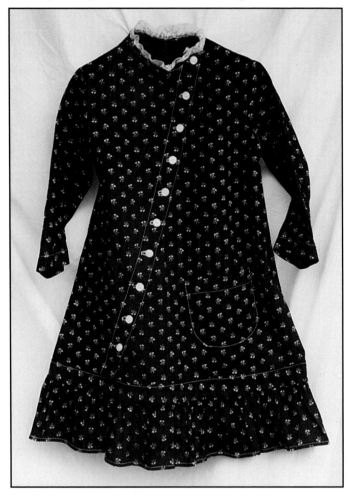

This boy's cotton dress is accompanied by a hand-written note: "This is a dress Mother was making for Wade when he died — about 1½ years old in November 1885." $65.00 – 85.00.

This c.1924 – 1925 pink cotton dress was purchased from the estate of a Hungarian woman who immigrated to the United States. The hand embroidery was created in her native country. $85.00 – 150.00.

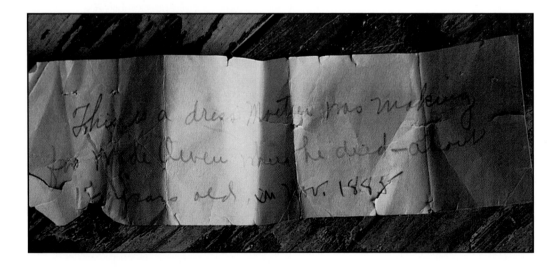

Princess Von Gotha of the House of Saxe-Coburg-Botha wore this capelet the evening she met her husband. Worn at a ball attended by Europe's royalty, this capelet is a rich mixture of silk, lace, ribbon embroidery, and ermine.
Without provenance, $100.00 – 175.00.
With provenance, $500.00 – 1,000.00.

Detail of Princess Von Gotha's capelet revealing fine lace and ribbon embroidery.

107

The Princess near the time she wore the capelet; the man is unidentified, but might be her fiancé Count.

The Von Gotha estate.

A postcard featuring the Von Gotha royal family.

The Princess, her American husband, and her daughter.

One of the many papers used to add documentation to the capelet: the Princess's birth certificate.

Chapter Sixteen

Organizing and Keeping Records of Your Collection

At one time or another, all collectors must deal with the problem of how to keep track of all their treasures. We start out well-intentioned (probably stashing our treasures in a very special chest or box), but it doesn't take long for our collection to begin overflowing. So, we buy a new box in which to store newly acquired treasures. You all know the end to this story. Before too long, we have somewhere between 10 and 1,000 boxes lying around the house — and in order to find just one very special treasure, we must dig through all the boxes...and, of course, what we're looking for is always in the last box. So I say again: at one time or another, collectors must face the problem of what to do with all their treasures.

Some people (and collectors are notoriously from this group) are happiest amongst the sweet pandemonium of disorder. I would not want to challenge any person's happiness, so if you are one of those people, you may wish to stop here and go on to the next chapter.

If, on the other hand, you are looking for peace and a solution, I will do my best to help you find it. It isn't necessarily easy. It may take a good weekend's work, depending upon how large your collection is and just how disorderly it has become. But, in the end, you will have not only order but good documentation of all your treasures.

Where to Start

A good place to begin is with coding; each individual piece in your collection should be tagged or labeled. This is not as horrible as it sounds. All that is necessary is to mark each piece with a number that's written on a piece of twill tape. One of the best ways to number is to create a code, beginning with the date of acquisition. For example, 95.12 means the item was acquired in 1995, the month of December. If you are a heavy-duty purchaser, you can even add the day: 95.12.29 (that is, 1995, the month of December, the 29th day); however, the exact date of purchase isn't necessary for the average collector. Most important is a code that tells you where you purchased the item. For example, the addition of the initials OF to any number in my collection means I purchased the item from a local vintage fashion shop called Old Friends. It's easy to devise your own codes for your own purposes — but keep a list of them in your record book. Finally, add to this an acquisition number; if this is the twenty-second item you've purchased for your collection, its code will be 95.12.OF.22.

Record book? Yes! This is, for me, one of the most enjoyable parts of the procedure. You know how grandmas keep a "brag book" of photos of their grandchildren to show to anyone who happens to be available? Well, your record book is going to be another sort of "brag book."

Your brag book can be as fancy or as plain as you like. Mine is simply a binder with 8½" x 11" paper placed in protective plastic sheets. I type up a record for each and every piece in my collection, like the example given in this chapter. I then place a photograph of the item on the same typed paper and place it inside the protective sheet. In addition, I may include a photocopied page from a current value guide that pictures or mentions a piece similar to the one I'm documenting. I sometimes also include a clipped page from an article that mentions the original owner of the piece, or some other pertinent information regarding the item. It's also a good idea to keep your receipts and insurance information in your record book.

And violà! You are done! It does take a

little time to document and organize a collection, but there are many rewards. First of all, any collection that is documented tends to be perceived as valuable by others who may eventually inherit or acquire it or a piece of it. It will also make the collection easier to appraise, and it will please your insurance agent. Documenting and organizing your collection also helps you focus on the course your collection is taking and when items you may want to look for in the future to better round-off your collection. My friend LaRee Johnson, who conducts fashion shows and lectures through her business Victoriana, tells me that she learned the value of coding or documenting a collection when she acquired another enthusiast's collection that numbered over 1,000. Though the woman from whom she acquired the collection had written notes on each piece, LaRee found it frustrating and time-consuming trying to match those descriptions with actual garments. Too, I know from personal experience that if you ever loan garments out for exhibits, it's extremely important to have each item labeled with a code to ensure its safe return to you.

Business-minded friends may ask, "What's the bottom line?" Documentation, organization, and research into your collection can actually increase the value of your collection — sometimes as much as ten percent! And not only that...it also makes your life a little more sane — and gives you a brag book to show off to friends! It doesn't get much better than that!

The Storage Problem

One of the most challenging aspects of collecting antique and vintage fashions is storage. Whether you're a museum curator, a private collector of many years, or a novice, the matter of storing vintage clothing in a safe and practical manner must eventually be tackled. The biggest problem collectors encounter when trying to develop a method of storage is space. Some fellow enthusiasts have written to me about their utopian storage facilities (much to my utter envy); one lady even had her husband build her a mini-museum in the back yard! Unfortunately, such conditions are only a fantasy for most collectors. The average collector, in fact, counts herself lucky if she can set aside a spare room for her collection (even if it must also serve as a

guest bedroom). But far more collectors are forced to "make do" with one closet here, a trunk there...

Preferably, all storage can be in one room, but if this is not possible, it's a good idea to keep garment types together in one room. (For example, all beaded 1920s dresses under the bed in the master bedroom, and all Victorian hats in the guest room closet.) Closets are usually the preferred area for storage in the home, but storage trunks and boxes are also suitable in conjunction with or separate from closets. Smaller items are often best stored in the drawers of narrow cabinets (like those designed for draftsmen and mapmakers). But whatever storage units you choose, they should be roomy enough to hold your collection comfortably (plus any new piece you'll be adding soon) and should be easy to get in and out of.

Hopefully, you will also manage to find room within your chosen storage area(s) for a large, flat table. This will encourage flat viewing of historical fashions and is essential for restoration activities.

Whatever space is set aside for storing your collection must be thoroughly cleaned and prepared before actually storing the garments. If there is carpeting in the area, it should be vacuumed; wooden floors should be swept and cleaned also. Walls should be wiped down, as should any wooden storage units. All of this will help prevent pests from feasting on your collection.

To protect your collection from acids that might cause stains, line any wooden storage units with unbleached muslin or old white sheets. Metal storage shelves or drawers should be padded with quilt batting at all pointed edges, then each drawer covered with muslin.

For future easy clean up, I've seen some collectors hang muslin on closet walls and floors (with Velcro); this, some collectors tout, makes you more apt to dust and clean your closets every few months, since all you have to do is throw the muslin liners into the washer and dryer. For added protection from dust, you can also add a strip of velvet or velveteen ribbon to closet or cupboard doors and cracks.

An ionizer (a little machine that actually sucks dust and other particles from the air) is a nice addition to the storage area. If you live in a moist or humid area, desiccating canisters are also a boon to your storage area; like the little packets found in shoe boxes, these canisters of "pebbles" will actually absorb excess moisture.

Flat Storage

Storing antique and vintage clothing on hangers is quite literally death by hanging. Whenever possible, historical clothing should be stored flat. This, unfortunately, takes up more space than hanging, but will ultimately prove less harmful to your collection.

The boxes used for flat storage are preferably archival-quality, acid-free boxes — but any strong box will do, as long as it is lined with unbleached muslin and acid-free tissue paper. Trunks will also work for flat storage — but again, they should be lined with muslin and acid-free tissue, and care must be taken that any sharp edges don't catch on the garments being stored. (In such cases, it may help to place a piece of cardboard — first covered with quilt batting, then with muslin — over the top layer of clothes.) Chests of drawers may also be used but must be lined with muslin and acid-free tissue to protect the garments from the harmful acids of the wood, chemicals of the plastic, or sharp edges of the metal.

Ideally, each piece of clothing should be stored in its own wide, long box or drawer. This leaves all but the widest, fullest garments free from folding (which can cause permanent creases and splits in some fabrics). Of course, this is utterly impractical. Most collectors will instead find that several garments must be stored in each box or drawer. Caution should be taken, however, to pack garments lightly into each box or drawer, since storing them together too tightly will create unnecessary wrinkles and may cause permanent creases. (By the way, all folds made in any garment while storing it flat should be well padded with acid-free tissue paper, in order to prevent permanent creasing.)

For the sake of sanity and order, place like garments together in boxes or drawers. (For instance, your three lingerie dresses in one box, and your 10 beaded blouses in another.) It's also a good idea to place the heaviest garments on the bottom of the box or drawer, with lighter garments resting atop. And always place a liner of unbleached muslin or acid-free tissue paper between each garment.

It's wise to note what's inside each box on a sticky-back label, which can then be placed on the most visible part of the box or drawer. Once your boxes are stacked neatly (inside the closet, under the bed, etc., it's also a good idea to make a quick sketch of where everything is located. These two simple measures will end needless rummaging through your boxes and drawers — which is not only messy but also frustrating.

Hanging Storage

Because hanging causes great strain on the shoulder, neck, and waist of garments, only the very lightest garments may be hung with any measure of safety. Lightweight blouses, undergarments, and some lingerie dresses fit into this category. Beaded or bias-cut garments definitely should not be hung (the first because they are too heavy, the latter because they will stretch out of shape).

Good hangers are essential. Regular padded hangers will do for some garments, but archival-quality hangers are best. Any hangers used should be amply padded, have no metal, plastic, or wood exposed, and put no strain on the shoulder, sleeves, neck, or waistline of the garment. It is advisable not to hang skirts, since they are usually on the heavy side; also, the only really good way to hang them is from their waistband, and this causes undue strain on that already fragile area of the garment.

Each item that is stored by hanging should then be covered in its own garment bag. Plastic will suffocate your collection (fabrics need to breathe in order to stay mildew free); white cotton garment bags are best, preferably without zippers — which might snag on and tear the garment.

Rolled Storage

Some smallish, flat items, (like shawls or handkerchiefs) can be stored rolled up, which saves an incredible amount of storage space. Any cardboard tube may be used for this purpose (if first covered with unbleached muslin or acid-free tissue), though specially made, acid-free tubes are also available from archival companies.

To store an item on a tube, first lay the item flat on a table, right side down. Then roll it onto the tube securely, but not tightly. Acid-free tissue should be inserted between each layer so that the item never touches itself. Once rolled up securely, wrap the entire tube in muslin and secure the end with a rust-proof quilter's safety-pin.

Small tubes can be easily stored in drawers or small boxes; longer tubes may be stuck under a bed or laid flat or upright in a closet.

Accessories

Rarely do vintage clothing collectors not own at least some fashion accessories. Here are a few tips for those sometimes hard to store items:

Shoes are best placed in shoe boxes (again, lined with muslin and acid-free tissue). Gently stuff each shoe with acid-free tissue paper to help keep its shape intact. (Shoe trees are not recommended, since they put undue stress on the shoes.)

Fans should be wrapped in muslin, then stored flat in a drawer or their own box. Museum curators disagree about whether fans should be stored open or shut — both states cause a certain amount of strain. Many curators store fans in a half-opened position.

Bags and purses should be gently stuffed with acid-free tissue, then wrapped in muslin, and stored together in smallish boxes (hat boxes work well).

And speaking of hats...hats should also be gently stuffed with acid-free tissue, then wrapped in muslin and boxed. Fragile hats should be stored on styrofoam heads.

Parasols are best stored half-opened (for the same reasons fans are), the insides stuffed loosely with acid-free tissue. If this is not possible, store the parasol closed — but in either case, the parasol should be kept in its own muslin drawstring bag. (The bag can then be hung by its drawstring, which is a great space-saver.)

Bustles and hoops don't necessarily fall into the category of accessories, but they are certainly tricky to store. Padded, cushion bustles can be stored in drawers or hatboxes, and small metal bustles should be stuffed with tissue and stored in their own box. Larger bustles and hoops, however, almost have to be hung. Sometimes the sturdy loops by which these articles were originally meant to be hung are still strong and supportive. If this is so, hang them from pegs in a closet. Otherwise, make your own loops out of muslin or store-bought binding; just make sure the bustle or hoop is well supported. If you have the room, collapse the hoops flat, wrap them in muslin, and store them thus. Thin metal hoops can be sandwiched between two layers of cardboard with three sides taped closed. In any case, storage under the bed or against the wall of a closet works well.

Acid-Free?

Regular tissue paper (the sort you generally use for gift-giving) is dangerous to your collectible fashions because it contains woody acids that will eventually produce yellow spots and stains. On the other hand, acid-free tissue, as its name implies, is free from those damaging acids. Fortunately, acid-free tissue is relatively easy to find at your local art supply store.

Acid-free boxes are also free from the chemicals that can damage fabrics but are more difficult to find. They can usually be purchased from one of the mail order companies that offer archival-quality products for family albums and paper collectibles, though the cost may be prohibitive for some collectors.

Regular cardboard boxes, however, can instead be lined with several layers of acid-free tissue and be entirely safe for your collection. Old sheets can also be used for this purpose, since they've been washed repeatedly and aren't likely to transfer dye to fabrics lying near them. Muslin works, too, and can be purchased for 50¢ to $1.00 a yard at a fabric store; just be sure to buy unbleached muslin and give it a good washing before you actually put it to use.

113

Sample Documentation Page

Garment: Bathing Suit, 2 pc. **Acc. No.** 94.10.DW.71

Era/Date: 1896 – 1905

Description: two-piece woman's bathing suit, consisting of a combination piece and separate skirt. Bloomers have elasticized bottoms and are attached to a bodice with buttons running up front, a sailor collar, and short cap sleeves. Sleeve ends, collar, and button placket are trimmed with rows of thin white braid. The separate skirt buttons to combinations at waistline and is trimmed with rows of white braid along waist and hem.

Fabrics: Wool

Source: Dorothy Wright, Eugene, OR, $70

Date of Acquisition: August 1995

Condition: Excellent.

Treatments: Hand washed

Restoration: None

Comments: This suit comes from the family of Dorothy Wright, though Dorothy isn't sure who originally owned it (was it her grandmother or her great-grand-mother?).

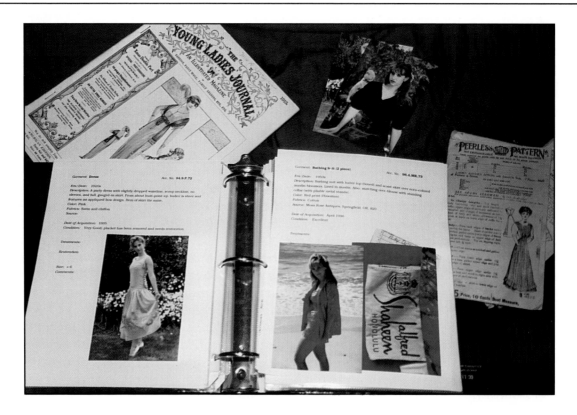

One of the author's documentation books. Waiting to be logged into it are photos of a dress and copies of patterns and fashion plates similar to items in her collection.

Chapter Seventeen

Labels

As collectors, we sometimes get caught in the label trap. Fantastic auction reports from elite auctioneers like Christie's and Sotheby's where so-called "designer" garments sell for thousands get our hearts pumping a beat or two faster when we spy a similar label in a vintage clothing shop. And yet the entire issue of "designer" clothes and labels is rarely discussed, even though it threatens many pitfalls for collectors.

First of all, the term "designer clothes" is a misnomer. All garments were designed by somebody, whether a local dressmaker, a ready-to-wear company, or a famous New York or Paris couturier. Typically what is meant by "designer clothes" is clothing created by the staff of a famous couture house like Dior or Chanel. But collectors should have some idea of the workings of these couture designer houses before blindly buying up anything with a couture label on it.

Before the mid-ninteenth century, there were no famous designers, just favored dressmakers who worked only for a small group of women of wealth and royalty. These dressmakers were invariably women, and it wasn't until an Englishman named Charles Fredrick Worth opened up a Paris dress business that "couture" was born. By chance, he found a client in a respectable princess, then a fashionable empress — and then his business was made. After Worth, there were others — Doucet, Poiret, even a woman named Paquin — but while their work was upheld as the best garment-making available, it was only available to an affluent few and was usually constructed by the staff, not by the couturier himself.

When in the 1920s the ready-to-wear industry began to boom, couture designers increasingly found themselves with less business on their hands, until by the end of the 1940s, coutures saved themselves by beginning to launch their own ready-to-wear lines.

Custom-made couture garments were still made, but mass-produced ready-to-wear made up the bulk of couture work, just as it does today.

Therefore, custom-made couture garments may sell for thousands at an elite auction; it is one-of-a-kind and has the prestige of having been created by a famous designer. But a ready-to-wear garment by the same designer has only a fraction of that value — it was produced in hundreds and has few of the special, detailed, often hand-applied details that a masterfully made custom couture garment does.

Bear in mind, too, that couture designers rise and fall from favor. One year, Chanel will be in demand, and her clothes from her early years will soar in value; but a few years later, demand for those same garments may diminish — along with their value — in favor of some other designer.

It's also important to remember that nearly all pre-1920s clothing is one-of-a-kind. Ready-to-wear did exist as early as the mid-nineteenth century for simple things like undergarments and, by the 1880s and 1890s, women's simple blouses and dresses. But contrary to what some people may imply, Victorian dresses rarely sell in the $1,000 range.

And are we to neglect the twentieth century ready-to-wear designers who fashioned the masses? It is their clothing that set real fashion, that laid down in history what the style of each period was.

Instead of allowing labels to rule us, collectors need to trust their instincts. I've seen Worth gowns from the 1870s that were sewn together as shoddily as a masquerade costume meant to be worn only once — and I've seen homemade garments that were exquisite. I've seen Chanel garments that were ugly as sin — and ready-to-wear garments that took my breath away. Labels don't dictate a garment's value.

Chapter Eighteen

Identification Tips For Women's Fashions

The following timeline is intended to help you identify and date exsisting authentic women's fashions. It should be used in conjuction with period fashion plates, period magazines, and books, since it highlights trends in general. Do remember that when a style first appeared, it was often considered too "fast" to be worn by many women; the average woman lagged behind "the latest" by about a year.

1800 – 1824

- Before c.1796, a good number of dresses are not new; rather they are old dresses altered into new styles. This trend continues (in a more limited way) well into the nineteenth and early twentieth centuries.
- One-piece dresses.
- Plain and printed cottons are popular; for evening, silk is most fashionable.
- White is extremely fashionable, as is yellow, and red accents.
- Piped seams are common after c.1822.
- Bodice is usually closed with tape ties and drawstrings in back.
- Hooks and eyes are used to fasten front-closing garments, and removable straight pins are also sometimes used as fasteners.
- Hooks and eyes may be brass, tin, or silver wire.
- A fabric tape tying around the waist may be attached to dresses at center back.
- Buttons made of metal rings covered with thread are worn occasionally from c.1800 – 1830.
- Necklines scoop low.
- By c.1815, day dresses usually have necklines ending at the base of the neck.
- Sleeves are long, straight, and plain by day, short by night.
- Short puff sleeves are worn over attached long sleeves after c.1810.

- Sleeves are gathered into the shoulder after c.1815, making them less fitted.
- By c.1815, sleeves are longer, covering the top of the hand.
- Petal-shaped sleeves are popular from c.1818 – 1820.
- Bodices are usually lined.
- Bodices and skirts have no boning.
- Bodice is usually gathered in back from c.1806 – 1822.
- Bib-fronts are seen after c.1810 — literally the front of the bodice is pinned on at the shoulder.
- Waistline is just below bust and is sometimes slightly higher in back.
- Waistlines are lower, only a few inches above natural, by c.1823.
- Skirts are fuller and may be gathered all around the waist by c.1823.
- Skirts are pleated or gathered tightly at back.
- Trains are worn for evening and day wear up to c.1806.
- Day skirts haven't a train after c.1806, but might be a little longer in back than in front.
- Padded hems are seen from c.1823 – 1828, especially in evening wear.
- Flounces or trim are often worn at the hemline after c.1810.
- Measurement all around the hem of dresses from c.1800 – c.1825 is about 36".

1825 – 1835

- Tie closures are rare by c.1830, except around the neckline.
- Armhole seam may have tape ties (usually three) from c.1825 – 1835; these are for attaching sleeve puffs to pouf out the top of the sleeve.
- "Imbecile" sleeves, full all around with most of the fullness at the shoulder and

gathered into a wristband, are worn from c.1829 – 1835.

- Sleeves are wider at top in the leg-o-mutton fashion from c. 1825 – 1836.
- Waistline is nearly natural — only slightly raised by c.1825; waistline is at its natural level by c.1827.
- Measurement around the hem is about 96" to 116" by c.1830.

1836 – 1840

- A hook with a stitched "eye" or bar is the most common closure by c.1836.
- Evening dresses may be laced up the back by c.1836.
- Bodices are boned (usually a bone at front, back, and sides) by c.1836.
- Sleeves are fitted, with a pouf at the elbow by c.1836.
- Sleeves are sewn onto the bodice at the upper arm.
- Skirts are usually lined.
- Measurement around the hem of skirts is about 125" – 144" by c.1835.

1841 – 1849

- Many garments are now stitched on a sewing machine.
- Two-piece sleeves appear; short ones attached to the bodice for evening wear, and long ones that may be attached to the short ones for day wear.
- A bone running from the neckline to the arm-hole (along the shoulder) is not uncommon after c.1840.
- V-necklines appear.
- Waistline is slightly pointed in front by c.1841.

1850 – 1869

- Nearly all garments are now stitched on the sewing machine.
- Popular trimmings include narrow ruching, small ruffles, fringe, braid or flat trim, and piped seams.
- Solid fabrics, especially taffeta silks, are popular. Many cotton and wool/cotton prints are also worn, as are border prints and plaids. Popular colors include black, white (for cotton blouses), royal blue, red, and grape.
- Geometric patterns, including those created

by trims, are favored.

- Hooks and eyes or buttons run down the front of garments; lacing is sometimes found running down the back of evening dresses.
- Padding between the bust and shoulder is often found on dresses from c.1850 – 1898.
- Sometimes two-piece dresses or skirts and blouses are worn.
- Two-piece dresses are more usual after c.1855, often with a bodice having a peplum.
- Many day bodices are not boned in the 1860s.
- Necklines are rounded at the base of the neck, but may scoop low for evening wear.
- Epaulets, or small cap sleeves worn over longer sleeves, are seen from c.1858 – 1860.
- Sleeves are set low on the shoulder, making shoulders look rounded and slightly drooping.
- Bell-shaped sleeves are popular, but sleeves are straight after c.1865.
- Watch pockets first appear in women's bodices.
- Bodices can sometimes be pointed in front and in back by c.1856.
- Waistlines are most often rounded by c.1860, though sometimes evening dresses still feature a V-waistline.
- Dresses sometimes have a slightly raised waistline by c.1860.
- Skirts are gauged, gathered, or sometimes pleated all around the waistline.
- The skirt is often folded over at the waistband, leaving a flounce on the wrong side of the skirt directly under the waistband.
- Skirts with many flounces are popular through c.1860.
- Skirts are flatter in front after c.1865, with most pleats, gathers, etc., in the rear.
- Skirts for evening can have a train by the 1860s.
- Overskirts appear c.1868.
- Measurement around the hem of skirts varies from 10 to 18 feet.

1870 – 1889

- Dresses are in two or three pieces: often bodice, skirt, and overskirt, and sometimes an additional overskirt.
- Dresses are generally one-piece and cut in the narrow princess line with puffs low in back, and often have long trains from c.1878 – 1881.

- The shelf-like bustle reappears c.1881.
- Two or more fabrics or colors are frequently used.
- Silks are common; also wool and velvet. Black is a common color, and wine, plum, brownish-red, royal blue, brown, forest and olive greens, and navy are popular.
- Trims are often fancy buttons, velvet binding, ruching, beading, and tassels.
- Hooks and eyes or buttons run down the front of day dresses, while closures may be in back for evening; lacing is still popular for evening dresses.
- Tapes sewn to the inside of bodices at the waist are common.
- Bodices are almost always boned.
- Sometimes built-in bustles are found in dresses from c.1870s – 1880s.
- Bodices are often jacket-like.
- Bodices often have a back peplum to emphasize the c.1870s bustle.
- Tight-fitting cuirass (corset) bodices with deep pointed waistlines are worn from c.1876.
- Collars are usually standing. Necklines can also be rounded or squared.
- High collars are especially popular from c.1880 – 1884.
- Sleeves are straight, but feature a slight puff at the shoulder after c.1887.
- Evening gowns can be sleeveless, but with wide shoulder straps from c.1876 – 1889.
- Underskirts usually have a plain or muslin center back, exactly where the next overskirt lies.
- Skirts are often fully lined by the late 1880s.
- Skirts are usually tightly gathered or pleated in rear.
- Skirts have inner tapes to help form the bustle and hold the skirt snug to body; by the 1880s, these are usually elastic.
- Skirt drapery is looped up over the hips after c.1883.
- Overskirts disappear generally after c.1886.

1890 – 1899

- Dresses are two pieces (prairie, reform, empire-revival, and maternity dresses may be one-piece).
- Silk is ever-popular; velvets, chiffons, and wools are also common. Bright colors like canary yellow, orange, and green are popular.

White becomes increasingly popular for summer wear, until by the late 1890s it is a staple. Pastels are also worn in the last few years of the 1890s.
- Bodices are well boned and fully interlined.
- Bodices fasten with hooks and eyes up the front or in front and along the sides; buttons are also used (especially for back closures).
- Bodice trimmings become more elaborate as the decade progresses: beading, ribbons, tiny ruching.
- Bodices sometimes have a lining with a separate fastening.
- The "pigeon-front" bodice begins c.1898.
- High collars are often worn and are sometimes separate from the bodice. Collars are boned with regular bodice boning, or with light metal wire, often in a zig-zag shape.
- Sleeves are tight with a slight puff at the shoulder until c.1893.
- Sleeves are in the very full, leg-o-mutton style from c.1894 – 1897.
- Sleeves revert to a slender style by c.1897, with only soft gathers or no gathers at the shoulder.
- Bodice and skirt usually hook together with a large hook and eye at the waistline.
- Skirts are interlined.
- Skirts have bindings of velveteen or braid on the inside of the hem to prevent wear.
- Hems are lined with stiff buckram or horsehair, from the bottom of the hemline to about 10" up.
- Skirts are relatively plain and trimmed only lightly; binding or braid is sometimes found at hemline.
- Skirts are ungathered or pleated, except at back.
- Skirts may have inner elastic bands to help control their folds in back.
- Trains reappear c.1890.
- An unusual find is the empire-revival, high-waisted dress.

1900 – 1909

- Chiffons, light cottons and silks, and lace are extremely popular. White is eminently popular, but pastels and black are also still popular.
- There are many fussy details: fine ruching, ribbons, insertions, tucks.
- Hooks and eyes are used on most dresses, but

snaps are sometimes sewn in-between.
- Dresses are often two-piece; after c.1905, one-piece dresses reappear.
- Bodices are always in the pigeon-front style.
- Bodice has a separate (but attached) lining, which fastens separately up the center front or back.
- Boning is minimal after c.1905.
- Sleeves are often looser or very full below the elbow.
- Evening dresses feature a slight empire-waist-line by c.1908.
- Separate belts, well-boned, are worn.
- Skirts are slender at the hips and flare at the hem.

1909 – 1919
- Day dresses are simpler and are usually one-piece.
- Satin, fine cotton, wool, and silk are popular, especially in shades of brown, red, blue, and gray.
- Evening dresses often feature metallic-shot lace or fabric, beading, and tassels.
- Snaps are used frequently; hooks and eyes continue to be used.
- Bodice boning disappears altogether after c.1917.
- Square necklines are especially popular for day wear, as are sailor collars.
- Collars are sometimes high and boned with celluloid strips.
- Suits consisting of skirt and jacket ending just below hip are popular.
- Waistline is slightly raised.
- Skirt is essentially tubular, without much full-ness, but wide, full-skirts are fashionable from c.1914 – 1915.
- Skirts for evening are trained and sometimes weighted.
- Skirts by day are shorter, tea length.
- The tube-like chemise dress appears c.1919, but is not generally worn until the next decade.

1920 – 1929
- One-piece dresses.
- Chiffons, light silk, and rayon are especially popular. Evening trimmings included rhine-stones and heavy beading. Bright colors were especially favored, including orange, greens, and yellows.
- Dresses often slip on over the head without fasteners or with a few hooks and eyes and snaps at the side.
- Dresses have no waistline or a dropped waist-line.
- The tubular, chemise dress becomes popular c.1920 – 1921.

1930 – 1939
- One-piece, long dresses are worn throughout most of this decade.
- Chiffons, velvets, cottons, and rayon are popular, especially in shades of royal blue, wine and burgundy, and peach. Black is also popular.
- Dresses usually fasten with snaps and hooks and eyes at side, but sometimes metal zippers on the side are seen after c.1939.
- Sweetheart necklines are common, especially for evening wear.
- Sleeves might have small, light shoulder pads after c.1936.
- Waistline is at its natural level and is often emphasized with an upside-down or right-side-up V.
- Bias cut skirts appear as a massive trend c.1929.

1940 – 1949
- One-piece dresses.
- Suits.
- Wool and cotton are favorite everyday fabrics, with satin and velvet often worn at night. Browns and blacks are particularly popular.
- Hooks and eyes and snaps or metal zippers are used on the side of dresses until c.1949, when metal zippers could sometimes run down the back.
- Skirts are short and narrow.
- A softer look emerges in 1947, with fuller skirts, peplums, long skirts, and (from 1947 to c.1950), padding, boning, and waistband tapes are used.

1950 – 1965
- Cotton and rayon are especially popular in bright colors.
- Bodices are fitted and snug.
- Skirts are full and either gathered or pleated to a waistband, or cut in the circle skirt fashion.

- A 1920s revival takes place from c.1960 – 1961, with dropped waists and chemise dresses sometimes being worn.

1966 – 1979

- The peasant, prairie, and Victoriana looks are popular.
- Pantsuits
- Plastic zippers begin to appear commonly from c.1968.

A c.1815 – 1820 hook and eye closure. The hooks are sewn onto a tape, which is in turn sewn to the inside of a drawstring waistline.

Detail of c.1850s gauging. Gathering stitches are taken by hand along the waistline of the skirt, then drawn up very tightly. From the outside of the skirt, these stitches are barely visible.

From the inside of the skirt, the stitches where the skirt is then attached to a waistband or bodice are clearly visible.

Hooks from a c.1860 bodice.

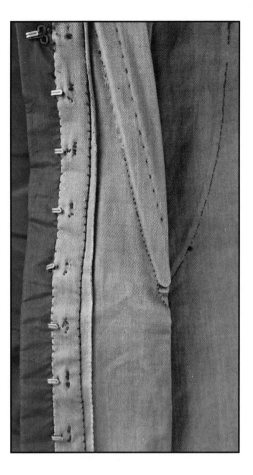

The inside of an 1860s bodice. Notice how the hooks that close the bodice in front are partially hidden beneath the fabric.

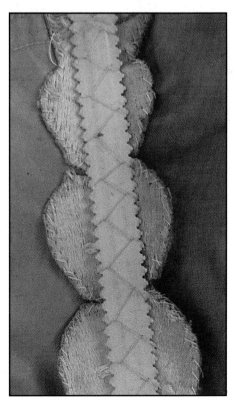

The inside of a finely crafted garment. The seams are scalloped and hand overcast to prevent raveling. The boning is encased in ribbon and hand sewn in place.

A tiny (barely ¼") painted porcelain button from a c.1900 bodice. Notice also the mixture of machine sewing (closest to the button and the braid trim) and hand sewing (on the opposite side of the photo).

121

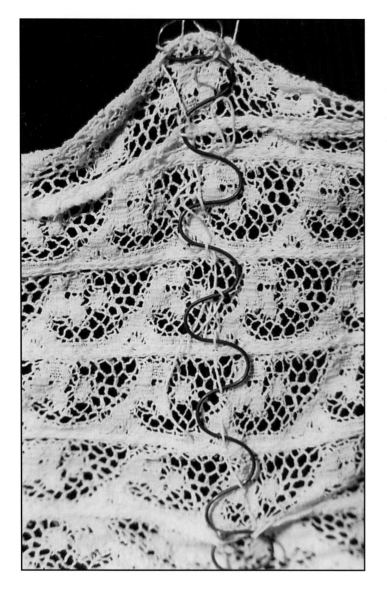

A wire "bone" inside the high collar of a c.1900 bodice.

A celluloid collar "bone" from a teens era bodice.

Chapter Nineteen

150 Years of Fashion: 1810 – 1960

Courtesy of Persona Vintage Clothing.

Early in the 1890s, jacket-bodices enjoyed brief popularity.
This one is rich silk velvet. $65.00 – 95.00.

Photo courtesy of Alan and Barbara King.

A classic turn-of-the-century portrait, featuring a lady dressed in the all-American shirtwaist.

A late 1930s – early 1940s dress. $30.00 – 60.00.

This early twentieth century ensemble includes an ivory silk shawl, white kid gloves, and a fan from China, all embroidered with flowers.
Shawl, $35.00 – 75.00.
Gloves, $25.00 – 45.00.
Fan, $20.00 – 40.00.

Photo courtesy of the Lassiter/Cheetham collection.

Fabulous hats from the 1890s.

This fashionable 1914 dress was available in pattern form for 15¢ from *The Home Book of Fashions.*

A flowing 1930s rayon dress with the backless, halter bodice that was so fashionable during this period. The apple-green stripes are appliquéd onto the plain white fabric. $45.00 – 65.00.

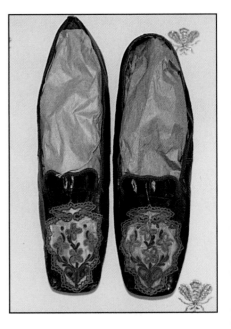

These patent leather party shoes date to c.1860 and are exquisitely embroidered. $150.00 – 250.00.

Photo courtesy of Karen Augusta.

Photo courtesy of LaRee Johnson collection.

A classic dress from c.1871. Many dresses of the 1870s – 1880s used striped fabrics creatively. $175.00 – 400.00.

Two early 1900s-era outfits. The brown dress is silk, worn with a felt hat and a fox muff. The gray silk dress is worn with a velvet hat.

Dresses, $95.00 – 150.00 ea.
Hats, $65.00 – 95.00 ea.

Photo courtesy of Alan and Barbara King.

Photo courtesy of Titiana Victoriana.

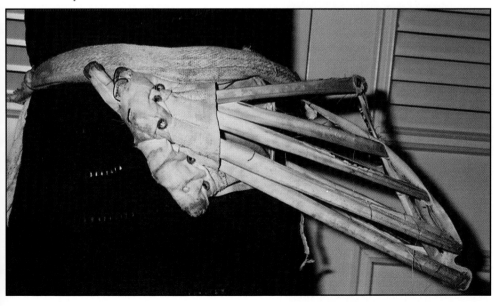

There were a myriad of bustle designs available in the late nineteenth century. This one, shaped something like a basket, is from the 1880s. $25.00 – 45.00.

This exquisite dress, c.1899, features a heavy, trained skirt. The separate bodice is faux-bolero style, with the vest, blouse, and collar all in one piece. $200.00 – 400.00.

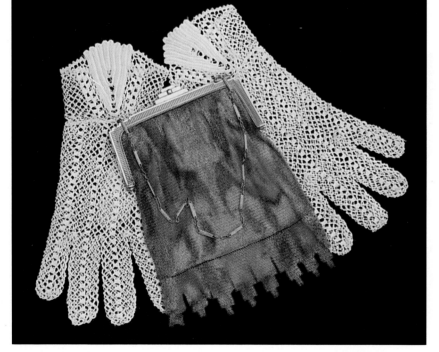

A multi-color metal mesh purse and crochet gloves, c.1920s – 1930s.
Purse, $100.00 – 200.00.
Gloves, $5.00 – 15.00.

Photo courtesy of the Lassiter/Cheetham collection.

Photo courtesy of the Lassiter/Cheetham collection.

A c.1910 white linen parasol with ivory tips, measuring 38" in diameter. $100.00 – 250.00.

An 1815 fashion plate, featuring a typical dress of the era: simply cut, but frilled.

Three typical women from the 1940s.

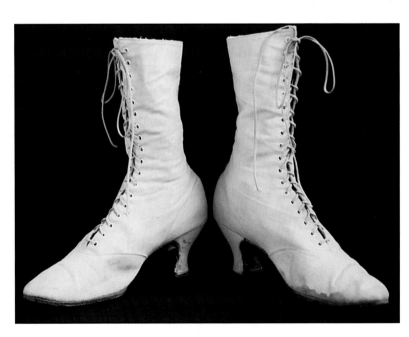

Linen hightop boots, c.1900 – 1909. $40.00 – 65.00.

129

Photos courtesy of the Lassiter/Cheetham collection.

This c.1913 – 1914 dress of white cotton woven with specks and stripes of pink and black features asymmetrical styling and a double skirt. The underskirt is of cotton voile trimmed with lace. The bodice neck is trimmed with ribbon roses and black tassels. $150.00 – 250.00.

In the 1890s, nearly-masculine styles became popular for women. This woman's suit is from 1893.

In the 1890s, there was a revival of empire-waisted dresses, similar to those worn in the early 1800s. Few women wore the style quite this costume-like and instead chose more typically 1890s headgear.

This well-boned c.1879 – 1882 silk evening bodice was called a "cuirass" (corset) bodice in its day. The low, V neckline is set off with tiny, etched metal buttons. The sleeves feature a flounced trim, and the "panniers" or hip panels are attached with hand-sewing. An attached bustle pad is sewn on in back. $100.00 – 175.00.

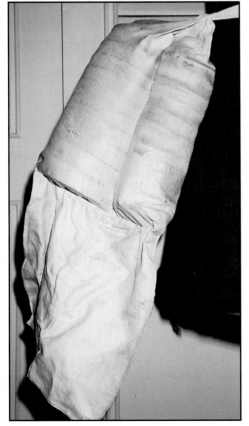

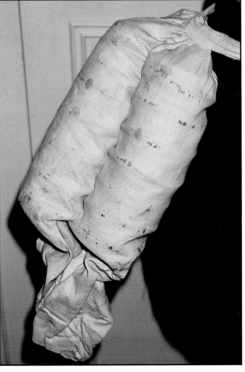

Two bustles from the 1880s, each using circular wires to form a protrusion. $35.00 – 65.00 ea.

Photo courtesy of Titiana Victoriana.

Photo courtesy of the Lassiter/Cheetham collection.

A two-piece dress from the early 1880s. The crisp cotton fabric features lavender and white pinstripes and is trimmed with varying widths of matching rose-print ribbon. $200.00 – 400.00.

Fox was an eminently popular fur in the 1890s, and capes like this one typified the first half of the decade. The tiny fox's head resting on the left shoulder of the cape is an artist's creation; it is entirely faked, though it was not uncommon for real heads to be included on fur garments. The muff is also of fox fur and is lined with satin. Cape, $30.00 – 65.00. Muff, $30.00 – 50.00.

An "evening gown for a bride." *Harper's Monthly* described it in 1854 as being fashioned out of moiré, covered almost entirely with white lace.

132

Up through the 1940s or so, women regularly mended their hosiery. This stocking mending kit from the 1920s was a giveaway and still contains a variety of silk threads and a fine needle. $10.00 – 25.00.

A basic 1930s evening gown pattern from Simplicity. $1.00 – 5.00.

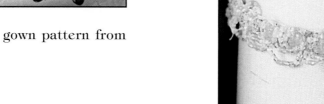

Elastic 1920s garters encrusted entirely with glass beads. $40.00 – 65.00.

Beaded "flapper" garters like this are a rare find. Dating to the 1920s, when frenzied new dances and shorter skirts might reveal garters, this set is elastic beaded solid with semi-precious stones. $85.00 – 150.00.

A parasol from 1870.

Photo courtesy of the Lassiter/Cheetham collection.

A c.1913 embroidered cotton blouse, shown with an ankle-length walking skirt. Blouse, $45.00 – 75.00. Skirt, $30.00 – 65.00.

Velvet evening gowns from the 1930s are relatively easy to find today, but vary enormously in style. This burgundy gown features ruching at the neckline and hips. $25.00 – 40.00.

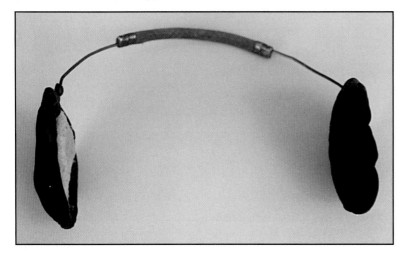

Kleinert's has made fashionable odds and ends for decades; these velvet ear muffs feature several patent dates, ranging from 1875 to 1885. $20.00 – 35.00.

A hand-sewn cotton dress, c.1840s. $200.00 – 300.00.

The rust-colored, striped dress dates to the 1890s, and the purple check silk taffeta dress from c.1863.
1890s dress, $100.00 – 250.00
1860s dress, $200.00 – 300.00

A lady of 1865, wearing a plain, hooped skirt, a lace trimmed blouse, holding a broad-brimmed hat.

A typical woman of the turn of the century, wearing a gored plaid skirt with a wide, shaped belt, and a shirtwaist.

This three-piece dress dates to c.1900. The gored silk skirt is trimmed with flounces and delicate silk ruching. The same ruching is found on the bodice front and sleeve ends. The white smocked front is attached, as are the velvet lapels and waistband. The collar, fashioned with white tucks and velvet, is separate. $200.00 – 400.00.

A smart costume from 1914.

An evening gown from the pages of *La Vie Parisienne* in 1923.

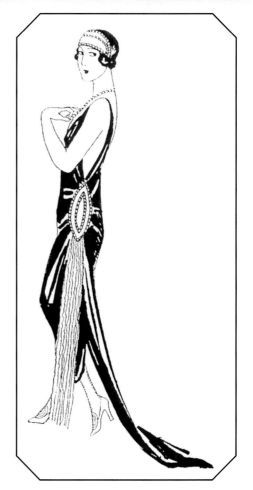

A velvet bag from the early 1900s, lined in royal blue silk. The plated silver top is in Art Nouveau style and features a mirror on the inside. $35.00 – 65.00.

This c.1825 gown is fashioned out of cotton and trimmed with satin. $700.00 – 3,000.00.

Photo courtesy of Karen Augusta.

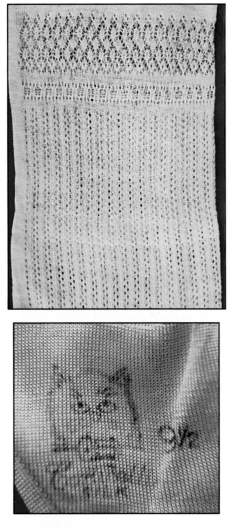

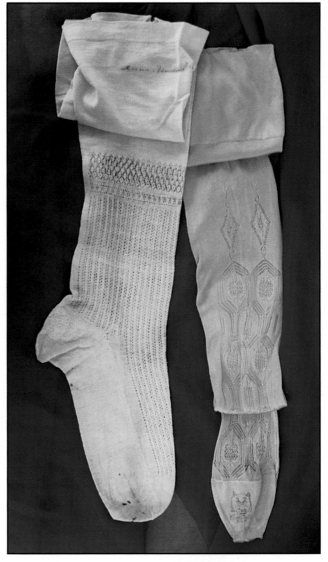

Two nineteenth century stockings. The white stockings probably date to the 1870s and are of cotton with delicate drawnwork decorating the tops of the foot, ankles, and shins. The cuff features a laundry mark with the original wearer's name in ink. The yellow stockings are silk and probably date to the 1890s. They feature the Corticelli Silk Company logo. White, $30.00 – 50.00. Yellow, $45.00 – 65.00.

A postcard from the early 1900s, displaying typical shoes and stockings of the period.

This smocked and lace-trimmed bodice was featured in an 1892 *Domestic Fashion Review* pattern catalog.

138

Two boudoir caps from the early 1900s. The blue cap is satin trimmed with hand crochet, and the pink cap is silk with lace insertion and ribbon roses on the crown. $10.00 – 25.00 ea.

The wrap-around style of fastening bodices grew increasingly popular as the twentieth century emerged. This bodice is a relatively simple example but is made distinct by its colorful shading. $25.00 – 40.00.

Below: At first glance these leather gloves are so detail-oriented, they appear to be Victorian. But a look at the inside stitching and snap closure reveals them to be c.1950s. $15.00 – 30.00.

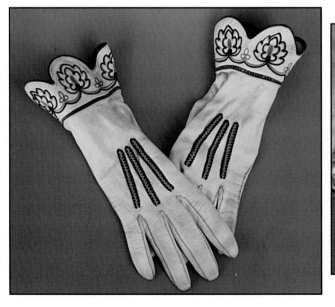

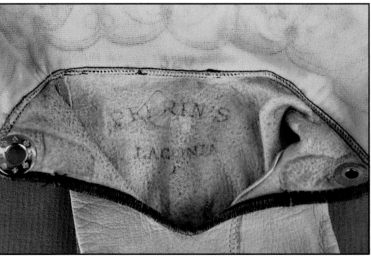

Photo courtesy of Alan and Barbara King.

An evening gown from 1815.

A fabulous 1930s crepe dress, shown with a fuchsia marabou jacket. Dress, $40.00 – 65.00. Jacket, $25.00 – 45.00.

A beaded bag from the early 1900s, featuring a metal clasp in a butterfly shape. $45.00 – 85.00.

This black silk dress trimmed with velvet and fringe was designed in 1874 by Worth, the most famous dress designer of the Victorian era.

Photo courtesy of Alan and Barbara King.

A 1960s green crepe Lili Anne suit with puffs of fur at the hem, worn with a feather hat. Suit, $15.00 – 30.00. Hat, $5.00 – 15.00.

This c.1890s – early 1900s black wool three-piece suit features a knee length, straight line, double-breasted coat with satin lapels and crocheted buttons. The woman's dress is c.1908 and is trimmed with lace and Irish crochet. Suit, $100.00 – 185.00. Dress, $90.00 – 200.00.

Courtesy of the Lassiter/Cheetham collection; photo by Steve Falconer.

Photo courtesy of the Lassiter/ Cheetham collection.

A classic suit from 1920.

This woman from the 1870s wears a snug velvet bodice ornamented by a small ruff and a large cameo.

A c. 1913 – 1914 lingerie dress, featuring a V-neck, a double skirt, dainty embroidery, and delicate details. The hat is of velvet, trimmed with silk flowers. $85.00 – 150.00.

A fashionable assortment from the 1840s – 1850s. The 1850s bodice of blue muslin is embroidered with delicate pink roses. The c.1840s – 1850s bonnet is of sheer cotton and is shaped with twigs.
Bodice, $65.00 – 120.00.
Bonnet, $95.00 – 200.00.
Shoes, $100.00 – 200.00.
Bag, $40.00 – 75.00.
Gloves, $10.00 – 30.00.

Photo courtesy of Alan and Barbara King.

Ruffs were very popular at the turn of the century and varied from feathered collars to pleated silk boas. These two ruffs were featured in the October 1905 issue of *The Delineator.*

By evening, scooping necklines and shorter sleeves were the vogue at the turn of the century. This simple yet elegant bodice features puff sleeves and delicate beading along the neckline. $30.00 – 50.00.

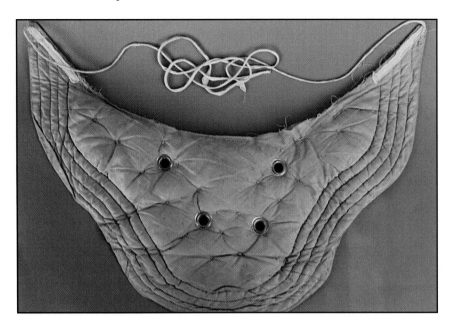

A bustle pad stuffed with horsehair. Sears catalog featured a similar one in 1908. $10.00 – 25.00.

In the early 1900s, women's dresses hovered between Victorian femininity and 1920s simplicity. This dress dates to 1915.

An early 1940s dinner dress with a shirred velvet bodice front panel; the remainder of the bodice is green silk net, decorated with fine green cording. $40.00 – 90.00.

Photo courtesy of the Lassiter/ Cheetham collection.

A classic 1940s dress, once available as a Butterick pattern.

An 1870 evening gown featuring an exquisite lace over-skirt.

This sheer chiffon blouse dates to 1910 – 1920 and is tucked, embroidered with pink thread, and beaded. $15.00 – 30.00.

In 1925, *The Fashion World* described this as "a gown with decided chic." The neck ribbon treatment was briefly vogue in the early 1920s and was called a "French tie."

This wool two-piece dress dates to c.1890 – 1894. The gored black skirt is trimmed with satin ribbon, and the bodice front and cuffs are trimmed with black braid. $175.00 – 275.00.

Stripes and polka dots were popular ways to showcase the fashion of wearing black and white color combinations at the turn of the century. This simple silk two-piece dress illustrates the earlier, less dramatic puffed bodice, pigeon-front look. The parasol dates to the early 1900s and is made of silk appliquéd with black lace. Dress, $75.00 – 100.00. Parasol, $100.00 – 200.00. Dress courtesy of Persona Vintage Clothing.

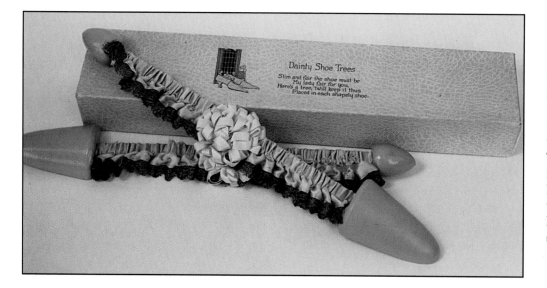

Shoes trees in their original box, dating to the early 1900s. The trees are made of silk-covered metal tipped with painted wood. The box reads "Slim and fair the shoe must be/My lady fair for you./Here's a tree, 'twill keep it thus/Placed in each shapely shoe." $30.00 – 50.00.

Photo courtesy of the Lassiter/Cheetham collection.

A beautifully tailored wool dress of c.1910 – 1912. The black lace collar and cuffs are lined with grape-colored silk and trimmed with black beaded fringe. $75.00 – 150.00.

Evening gowns from 1835.

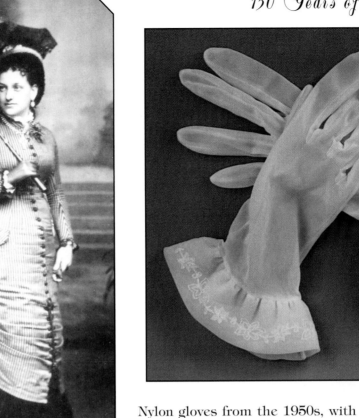

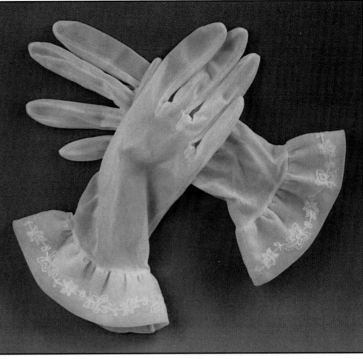

Nylon gloves from the 1950s, with dainty machine embroidery. $3.00 – 10.00.

A fashionably dressed lady from c.1879 – 1880.

A striped evening gown from 1860.

A rare outdoor portrait of a young woman of the 1890s wearing a simple gored skirt with a tucked bodice featuring wide insets of lace.

149

Photo courtesy of Alan and Barbara King.

An early 1900s dress of silk satin trimmed with black lace. $200.00 – 300.00.

A romantic, early 1900s evening wrap, from a Butterick sewing pattern.

An ostrich feather fan c.1890s – early 1900s, approximately 28" wide. The sticks are celluloid imitating tortoise shell. $65.00 – 75.00.

This two-piece dress from c.1892 – 1893 features a gored skirt topped off with a separate, asymmetrical bodice. The neck fill at center front is pink silk, and half of the bodice and the upper portion of the sleeves are brown silk. The other half of the bodice and lower sleeves are a heavy, upholstery-like lace. The bodice closes with hooks and eyes down the front. The faux-buckle closure is faceted metal. $175.00 – 350.00.

A c.1890s belt of boned cotton with extensive braid trim. $10.00 – 25.00.

Photo courtesy of the LaRee Johnson collection.

A typical dress from 1914.

A dress from 1922.

A classic silk bias cut gown from the 1930s. $95.00 – 195.00.

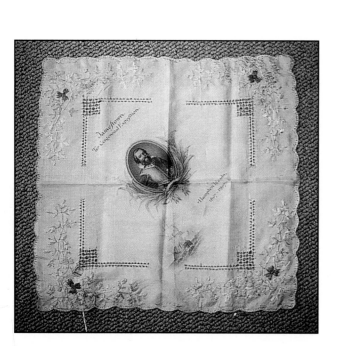

A commemorative silk handkerchief. $35.00 – 70.00.

Photo courtesy of Alan and Barbara King.

A rayon blouse from the late teens – early 1920s. The front features lace insertions set off by ruching, and the sleeves are trimmed with cording and a ruffle. $10.00 – 30.00.

This pink chiffon dress dates to the 1920s. $45.00 – 85.00.

A magnificent skirt from the early 1900s. Fashioned from striped cotton, it features V-shaped tucks and Battenburg lace insets. $100.00 – 200.00.

Photo courtesy of the Lassiter/ Cheetham collection.

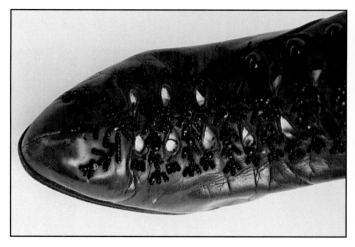

These black leather shoes feature cutwork from toe to ankle, trimmed with sparkling jet beads. Each boot has 12 tiny buttons and buttonholes. $110.00 – 185.00.

Photo courtesy of the Lassiter/Cheetham collection.

The shoes above can be dated by this photo found in a 1906 fashion magazine.

A stunning early 1910s silk parasol in slate blue shades. It measures 44" in height. $150.00 – 250.00.

Courtesy of the Lassiter/Cheetham collection.

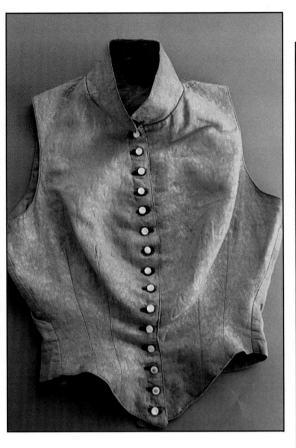

Photo courtesy of the LaRee Johnson collection.

A ladies' vest from the 1890s. The back and lining are plain booking cotton; the front and mandarin collar are brocade with touches of pink. The buttons are mother-of-pearl. $20.00 – 40.00.

A classic 1930s dress.

A late 1890s dress trimmed with black and ecru lace. $150.00 – 300.00.

This black lace fan mounted onto a mother-of-pearl frame and handpainted with flowers came from Spain in the 1950s. The gloves trimmed with beaded fringe date to the same era. Fan, $20.00 – 60.00. Gloves, $5.00 – 10.00.

Photo courtesy of the Lassiter/Cheetham collection.

A young misses' evening gown, c.1815 – 1820, cut with a slim skirt, a high-waisted bodice gathered at center front, and cap sleeves trimmed with lace, braid, and decorative buttons. The handsewn gown closes in back with one hook and eye at the neck and another at the waist. $600.00 – 1,000.00.

Courtesy of Vintage Silhouettes

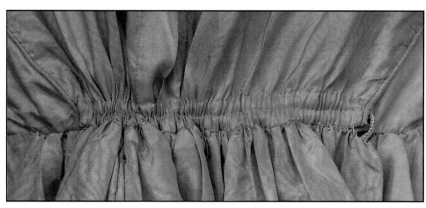

A waistline drawstring creates tight gathering at center back and further secures the gown shown on the previous page.

Beginning c.1892, high-waisted dresses (harkening back to the fashions of the early 1800s) could be fashionably worn instead of normally-waisted dresses. Both of these designs appeared in an 1893 issue of *The Delineator;* the dress with the front ribbon trim was dubbed a "house gown."

Simplicity in cut, with striking details, was the epitome of fashion in the 1930s and 1940s. This crepe eveing dress features colorful parrots. $75.00 – 120.00.

Photo courtesy of LaRee Johnson collection.

An early 1900s era suede bag with black suede appliqués garnished with jet beading. The round top is celluloid. $70.00 – 95.00.

This exquisite turn-of-the-century cotton bodice features handstitched faggoting, along with the puffed-out pigeon-front look. $60.00 – 75.00.

158

This ensemble could be purchased in the form of a Butterick pattern in 1905.

A one-piece dress, c.1858 – 1863. This homemade dress features epaulets of black fringe and an unusual lace trim in front. The pagoda sleeves are lined in pink silk; the white undersleeves are reproductions. $100.00 – 200.00.

An exquisite early 1900s era bodice of velvet and chiffon with beaded accents, worn with a gored skirt. The hat is straw and the parasol linen. Bodice, $45.00 – 70.00.
Skirt, $30.00 – 40.00.
Hat, $100.00 – 200.00.
Parasol, $95.00 – 200.00.

Photo courtesy of Alan and Barbara King.

An early 1900s photo of a woman wearing an exquisite crochet and lace bodice.

Two styles of Victorian suits for women. The riding habit, complete with masculine-inspired tie, collar, and hat, dates to 1894. The second outfit, whose only masculine influence seems to be a walking stick, dates to 1904.

Photo courtesy of the Lassiter/Cheetham collection.

Photo courtesy of Alan and Barbara King.

Peacock motifs were popular in the 1920s – 1930s, when this silk fan embroidered with gold thread was created. Bodice, $55.00 – 95.00.

This yellow chiffon dress dates to c.1915. Bodice, $75.00 – 110.00.

This 1930s dress is fashioned from a very pale peach rayon, machine embroidered with strawberries. The shaped waistband, puff sleeves, and collar are all typical of the period. $25.00 – 45.00.

A simple party frock from 1923.

A late Victorian parasol of white eyelet, measuring 30" in diameter. $100.00 – 125.00.

Photo courtesy of the Lassiter/Cheetham collection.

Vividly colored fashions are an exceptional find for today's collector. This stunning 1890s pink bodice of silk velvet reflects the Art Nouveau influence of the period; curving, elegant blades of grass are depicted with carefully stitched braid and embroidery. $85.00 – 125.00.

Assorted ladies' shoes, from the 1840s – 1860s. $100.00 – 200.00 ea.

Photo courtesy of Karen Augusta.

Photo courtesy of Karen Augusta.

A c.1839 gown, shown from the back. The sleeves are set low on the arm and are tightly pleated and stitched down at the top, while they balloon out at the bottom. $300.00 – 600.00.

Fashions of the early 1800s.

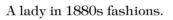

A lady in 1880s fashions.

Photo courtesy of the Lassiter/Cheetham collection.

This c.1890 – 1891 two-piece dress is made stunning by its fabric, which is black cotton sprigged with a floral pattern. $150.00 – 350.00.

Two evening dresses from 1892.

A c.1910 – 1912 blouse with lovely royal blue embroidery accents. $65.00 – 95.00.

Photo courtesy of the Lassiter/Cheetham collection.

Two party dresses from 1914.

Photo courtesy of the Lassiter/Cheetham collection.

A 1930s silk velvet jacket featuring flowing sleeves; it is worn over a bias cut silk chiffon dress. $75.00 – 100.00.

A typical dress pattern from the 1930s.

"Dressy Autumn Styles" from a 1906 fashion magazine.

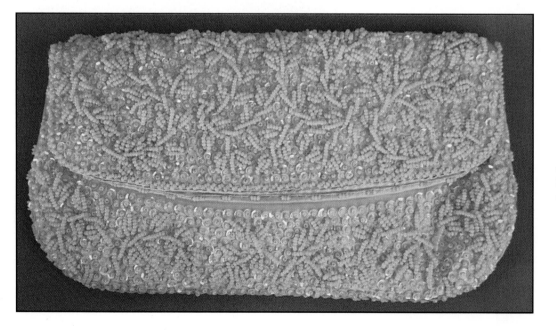

A beaded evening bag from the 1950s. $10.00 – 15.00.

Two fashionable young
women of the 1890s.

A wildly colorful silk
dress from the 1920s.
$65.00 – 95.00.

This rayon dress
dates to the 1940s; it
is homemade, and
like many dresses of
the period, though it
is relatively plain, it
has attractive details.
In this case, the
dress is appliquéd
with three-dimen-
sional bows. The
dress was said to be a
bridesmaid's outfit.
The black felt hat is
also from the 1940s
and is trimmed with
wired velvet roses.
Dress, $20.00 – 35.00.
Hat, $25.00 – 35.00.

A blue jersey bodice embroidered with metallic thread in multi-colored tints, from an 1888 issue of *Harper's Bazar.*

A fashionable 1880s lady from the pages of *Godey's Lady's Book.*

McCALL PATTERNS (All Seams Allowed)

2442, LADIES' SHIRT WAIST.
PRICE, 15 CENTS

2467, LADIES' OVER-BLOUSE.
PRICE, 15 CENTS

2441, LADIES' BLOUSE WAIST.
PRICE, 15 CENTS

THE VERY NEWEST IDEAS FOR WINTER WAISTS

FOR DESCRIPTIONS, SEE OPPOSITE PAGE

Ladies' shirtwaists, available in pattern form for 15¢ each from *McCall's* in 1908.

Fashionably dressed ladies from a 1905 issue of *The Delineator.*

An evening dress from 1864.

Appendix

At book signings, lectures, and museum exhibits, historical fashion enthusiasts often ask me questions about our favorite subject. Over the years, some questions have been repeated often enough that I thought it prudent to include them here.

"I am a beginning collector and wonder just what is available these days. Can I really expect to find the sort of things I see in this book at my local vintage clothing store or through mail order sources?"

For the most part, yes. This is not to say that you're going to find a dress or a pair of shoes or a hat precisely like the ones shown here, but you can find similar items. Here's a quick run-down of what's most available to today's collectors:

Women's Clothing — Women's undergarments, including petticoats, drawers, corset covers, and shifts — elaborate and simple — are extremely plentiful. Slightly less plentiful, but still easy to find, are corsets, hoops, and bustles. Pre-1920 underclothing is easiest to find. Women's outerclothing from the 1860s forward is in plentiful supply; only a few dress styles from the 1860s forward can be considered "rare." In this category, too, are capes, mantles, coats, jackets, and other protective or decorative garments. Unless in a shade other than black, these are also very abundant.

Men's Clothing — Men's fashions have either not survived (or been saved) as much as women's, or dealers tend not to present them as abundantly. Articles of men's clothing from the 1860s forward are most plentiful, with articles from the 1890s forward seen most often. It's rare to find complete suits intact.

Children's Clothing — Babies' long white gowns and robes, christening gowns, and bonnets — both simple and elaborate — are abundant. Often these items were saved in trunks for future generations or simply for sentimental reasons. Older children's clothes are often more difficult to come by — unless they were for special-occasion wear — because they wore out relatively quickly compared to adults' clothing. Again, whites are plentiful, and clothing from the 1890s forward is abundant.

Accessories — These follow many of the same trends as clothing, with children's accessories being slightly more rare. Shoes from the 1890s forward are plentiful, even in excellent condition. Hats from the 1850s forward are also abundant, and gloves are so common that many dealers won't stock them. Many people have great difficulty dating gloves and since most gloves seen on the market today date from 1900 forward, it pays to be an informed shopper. Fans have become a specialty and are often very expensive, especially if from before the 1860s. Again, many people tend to date fans to a period earlier than their true origin. Purses of all sorts are available, though most date to the 1880s or later. Most popular (and quite abundant) are beaded bags, which usually date to the 1920s.

"I've always heard that vintage clothing should be stored and wrapped in acid-free tissue, but when I tried to buy some, I was confused about the difference between buffered and unbuffered acid-free paper. What's the difference?"

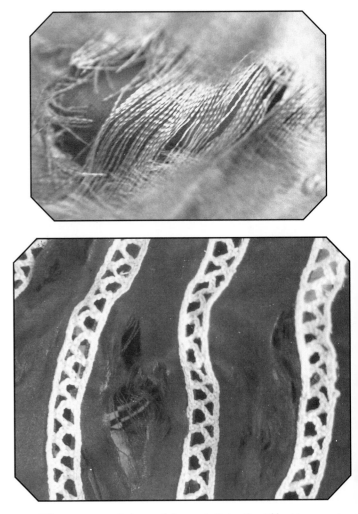

The difference between buffered and unbuffered acid-free tissue paper is minimal but significant. Unbuffered tissue is free from chemicals that are harmful to fabrics, increasing their rate of deterioration, causing yellow spots to appear, and holding soil into the garment's fabric. Buffered tissue also meets this criteria plus it neutralizes acidic gases and pollutants from the atmosphere. For this reason, it isn't necessary to throw away used buffered tissue and replace it with fresh paper as often as it is with unbuffered acid-free tissue paper.

The decision of which type of acid-free tissue to use is mostly a question of personal preference; however, buffered tissue is not suitable for (and will actually cause harm to) silk and wool fabrics.

"I've heard some really scary rumors about weighted silk. Is it really dangerous? And how can I know if I have any in my collection?"

The first step toward avoiding the hazard of weighted silk is to learn to recognize it. Speaking simply, weighted silk is a type of silk fabric that has metallic particles (including lead and arsenic) added to it to increase its weight and texture — making it appear more expensive. Fortunately, since the 1940s, garments made in the United States have only been allowed a 10% weighting (considered safe) and must be labeled as such. In order to identify weighted silk from earlier periods, however, you must learn to recognize what unweighted silk feels like. Go to a fabric shop that specializes in special occasion and bridal fabrics and have a salesperson show you a variety of silks. Handle them, noticing their texture and weight. Once you've done this, identifying vintage or antique weighted silk should be fairly easy — it will feel heavy and will most likely appear shredded and deteriorated. Too, most antique and vintage weighted silks have at least some "shattering" *(see above photos)*, a special type of disintegration that appears only on weighted silks.

If you want to add weighted silk items to your collection (and there's no real health reason that you shouldn't), or if you already have weighted items in your collection, handle them wearing white cotton gloves. (As a rule of thumb, you should do this with all your collectible clothing to avoid getting them soiled, but use a separate pair of gloves for your weighted items.) It's also important to separate weighted garments from non-weighted garments by storing them in a separate box, or in a special section of your closet, separated by a white cotton sheet. Don't allow the weighted silk to touch itself, since this increases the fabric's deterioration process; pad all fabric folds generously with unbleached muslin.

It isn't wise to wear weighted silk garments — not only because they could be harmful to you if you wear them for a length of time, but also because you are harmful to the delicate state most silk vintage clothing is in. As far as cleaning weighted silk is concerned, vacuuming the garment with a handheld vac whose head has been covered with cheesecloth is the best treatment; dry cleaning will only make the garment more brittle and more prone to deterioration.

"Often when I hear about how to care for vintage clothing, it seems that pre-twentieth century items should be handled more carefully. Are nineteenth century clothes more fragile than twentieth century clothes?"

Not necessarily; if a nineteenth century (or earlier) garment has been in an ideal environment, it may be much stronger than a twentieth century garment that has been stored in someone's basement for years. Many other factors also affect the condition of collectible clothing, including whether or not it has ever been worn (the more it was worn, the less likely it is to be in good condition), what sort of treatment the original manufacturers gave the fabric (for instance, some nineteenth century gowns were treated with metals that eat away at fabric), and how well-made the garment is.

If people seem to handle nineteenth century clothing a bit more cautiously, it's probably because such clothing is becoming rarer by the moment. Proper care and handling of all antique and vintage garments will help keep these important historical "documents" alive for future generations to enjoy.

"My mother always considered and taught that women's and children's fashion are art forms, truly an art if done with aesthetic inspiration; I feel the same way. I wonder how you feel about this."

Early in the days of studying historical fashions, this viewpoint was common; fashions were considered collectible and worthy of study because of their artistic value. In the struggle to have fashions be taken seriously as historical artifacts, however, this view is now largely put aside — it seems, at least by outward appearance, to apply only to couture designer (and leisure class) garments. Most costume historians today focus on a much wider variety of clothing; not just what was worn by the wealthy, but what was worn by everyone — right down to the tattered garments of a slave.

Nonetheless, we cannot ignore the fact that people of the past (until rather recently) considered it the duty of women to dress themselves in a tasteful manner. "Artistic" qualities in dress were often discussed in nineteenth and early twentieth century fashion journals. (And, as you state in your letter, women often applied these same "artistic rules" to their children.) First, a woman was expected to dress well and "artistically" to attract a husband and to represent her father in a good light. Later, the similar "duties" of representing her husband with her children's and her own "artistic" dress was considered important.

Unfortunately, in the midst of growth into the serious study of historical fashions, thinking of costumes in artistic terms has become somewhat passé.

"I have just finished reading your book Victorian & Edwardian Fashions. *How old are the models in your book compared to the women who would have worn the dresses originally? I was told that most Victorian dresses are too small for women of the same size today."*

Many rumors (mostly false) about the tiny size of Victorian women have been circulating for years. First, it's important to remember that dress size is relative. Even today, two size 8 dresses are not identical in measurements — so imagine what a difference there is between today's size 8 and a size 8 from 50 or more years ago! Too, standard sizing (like dress sizes 6, 8, 10, etc.) is a relatively modern invention.

The models I photographed for *Victorian & Edwardian Fashions* and, generally for the book you're reading now, ranged in age from 13 to 30 and varied in modern dress size from 4 to 12. I have seen extremely tiny Victorian adult clothes and I have seen rather large Victorian garments (including an 1840s corset with a waist of 40+ inches!). Still, it is certainly true that many women's Victorian clothes discovered by today's collector seem quite small in comparison to modern women. The reasons for this are varied.

It is true that people had a tendency to be smaller in the past (due in part to lack of good nutrition and bad health habits — not to mention, in the case of women, corseting from a young age, and, in general, inactivity). But it is also true that the clothes that have survived aren't always a good representation of the woman of the past.

The antique garments that are now in the finest condition were tucked away in attic trunks — perhaps because they were worn on a special occasion (like a first dance, a graduation, or a confirmation). Very often, clothes that had been outgrown by young women (either because of aging and growth or because of pregnancy) were kept. (They thought, just as many young women do today, that they'd be able to fit into them again soon after the baby.) In addition, as clothing styles change, smaller clothes are much more difficult to re-cut into newer styles than most larger garments are. All of this, coupled with the fact that nineteenth century people saved clothing far more frequently than we do today, accounts for the wide availability of small-ish Victorian garments.

"It seems I never find garments with labels in them. (I collect clothes and accessories from the 1920s through the 1940s.) Does this mean everything I buy was homemade?"

It is downright uncommon to see labels in antique or vintage clothing from before the 1940s. It is true that some of these unlabeled clothes were, indeed, homemade, but many ready-to-wear, dressmaker-made, and even designer-made fashions went without labels during the eras you mention.

Some garments started out with labels, but these were later removed because they annoyed the wearer (surely a more common occurrence then than now — women weren't used to labels). More commonly, however, labels were removed by sales shops and departments stores, which was legal at the time.

The only way to tell homemade garments from ready-to-wear garments is by examining details on the inside of the garment. Hand-stitched seams and handfinishing (such as hand-overcast seam allowances, and carefully hand-sewn hems) almost always indicate the garment was home-made or made by a dress-maker. Still, unless the quality of sewing is less than excellent, such handsewing could also indicate the garment was from a couture designer.

"Why do you recommend using Neutrogena face wash for washing vintage clothes? Why would you use a beauty bar on old clothes?"

First, let me say that antique or vintage clothing should never be washed if it is not noticeably dirty. Even then, other options (such as brushing or vacuuming) should be explored before washing is tried, since wet fabric is always weak fabric.

However, if you find that certain garments must be washed in order to be preserved (and if you find, after a test on an inconspicuous spot, that the garment is safe to wash in water), special, gentle cleansers should be used. Unfortunately, this leaves out most soaps and detergents used today. (Even those marketed as "gentle" are too harsh for old fibers.) Therefore, professional conservators recommend using a product called Orvus. But Orvus (usually found in fabric stores under the brand name "Quilt Care") is often difficult to locate.

There is a solution, however — and one that the Smithsonian Institution has been using for years: Neutrogena face wash soap. It is gentle, non-abrasive, and easy to find at any drug store. Always use the "original formula," and dissolve about ⅛ of a 3½-ounce bar in one cup of water, and add this to approximately every gallon of washing water.

"Why were some Victorian dresses given the label "visiting dress" as opposed to "tea dress?" Or "dinner dress" as opposed to "evening dress?" How did Victorians make these distinctions when to me the dresses look equally formal or casual (i, Victorian dresses could ever be casual!)?"

Your question is not an easy one to answer. Probably the reason you have not found the answer in any book (and, as far as I know, the subject is not covered in any book) is precisely because it's so complicated to decipher the old Victorian codes of dressing.

While it would take reams of paper for me to answer your question in detail for each era, I can give you an explanation using turn-of-the-century dresses as an example; you can then apply the same ideas to other eras. For the most part, the distinguishing feature between a walking, dinner, visiting dress, etc., was hem length, and neckline, and sleeve style. This was rarely pointed out in fashion magazines of any era, since it was considered general knowledge, but a 1905 issue of *The Delineator* did make some points that might be useful to you:

"In determining the fashionable length of the season's dress skirts, the style of the gown and the occasions upon which it is mostly likely to be worn should be considered. For street wear three lengths are provided — instep, short round or clearing, and round. In instep the length of the bottom of the skirt is two inches from the floor, and this length is a favorite for general utility wear. Naturally a gown of this length will be rather simple in style and generally on plain tailor-made lines. It is suitable for morning and for shopping and is essentially a walking skirt or, as the French gown-makers have named it, 'trotteur,' a title which particularly well describes its very useful qualities.... *(this length is shown in Figure 1)*...and is suitable for outing wear and for golf though not necessarily confined to these uses.

"The skirt one inch longer is said to be in short round or clearing length, as it clears the floor by one inch...(This) is shown in *Figure 2*. This is the favorite length for shirt-waist gowns and street wear.

"The dressy tailor-made gown for calling or afternoon wear is best liked in what is called "round" length. This touches the floor at front, sides and back...The model shown in *Figure 3*...(was) developed in fine broadcloth of a light color (and can) become, by the addition of appropriate trimming, a gown suitable for the most formal occasion...

"The medium sweep *(Fig. 4)* and the long sweep *(Fig. 5)* are suitable only for house gowns or for wear when no outdoor walking is to be done. The skirts of both touch the floor in front and at the sides. *Figure 4*...has a train or sweep measuring six inches, while *Figure 5* measures 10 inches. This is quite as long a train as is worn on ordinary evening dress.

"For the skirt of a wedding-gown a train of extra length is cut, and this is seen in *Figure 6*...The length is two and one-fourth yards from the belt to the end of the train."

Figures 1 & 2

Figure 3

FIG. 1—INSTEP LENGTH.   FIG. 2—SHORT ROUND LENGTH.

FIG. 3—ROUND LENGTH.

Figure 4

Figure 6

FIG. 4—MEDIUM SWEEP.

FIG. 6—FULL TRAIN LENGTH.

Figure 5

FIG. 5—LONG SWEEP.

Now, you can imagine that while it might be fairly easy to measure train lengths, it is nearly impossible to tell the difference between a dress that originally ended one inch above the floor and a dress that actually touched it — you would need to put the dress on the woman who originally wore it in order to determine this. So now sleeve and neckline styles must be taken into account. For example, during any particular era were long (to the wrist) sleeves always worn by day, though by morning sleeves ending at the elbow were more fashionable? Were high boned necklines always worn by day and only evening gowns revealed the neck and bosom?

I suggest that you consult some books that show many period fashion drawings (along with their original descriptions) in chronological order. *Victorian Fashions & Costumes from "Harper's Bazar," Fashions & Costumes from "Godey's Lady's Book," Paris Fashions of the 1890s, Women's Fashions of the Early 1900s,* and *59 Authentic Turn of The Century Fashion Patterns* may be good choices for this purpose (see the bibliography for details). Study these period pictures and compare them with the captions (which will identify them as visiting dresses, dinner dresses, etc.); it will take some time, but you can learn to decipher the Victorian code of dress if you watch carefully for details.

Afterword

The world of collectible fashions is a widely varied one. No one could ever write a single book that would encompass all aspects of this ever-growing field, but this book, I hope, has given you a good basis for starting or continuing to build your own collection. I hope it has also introduced you to areas, ideas, and inspirations you may not have been familiar with before.

The single most important thing I hope you've gleaned from this book is that the world of collectible fashions is one of constant learning and growth. The field is fairly new, and all of us — from the novice collector, to the museum curator, to the historical expert — are still learning constantly. I'd be delighted to hear from you about your own discoveries, your questions, and your concerns about collectible fashions. It is through interaction that we will gain the most knowledge.

Please write to me, if you wish. You can send letters and photographs to me in care of the publisher of this book.

In the meantime, protect and cherish your collection — those are the only standards that will earn you the proud title "Vintage Fashion Collector."

About the Author

Kristina Harris is one of the most widely published experts in the field of antique and vintage fashions; she has written on the subject for nearly every antiques-related publication produced in the United States, in addition to such magazines as *Woman's Day* and *Victorian Decorating & Lifestyle.* She is the former editor of the national newsletter for *The Costume Society of America,* the clearinghouse organization on fashion; she's also the editor of the internationally distributed historical fashion collector's newsletter, *Vintage Connection.*

Kristina is an enthusiastic lecturer and workshop director on subjects related to historical fashions. An avid women's history and fashion aficionado, Kristina guest curates museum exhibits on the West Coast.

Other Books by Kristina Harris

The Child In Fashion (Schiffer, 1998)
Vintage Fashions For Women: the 1950s & 60s (Schiffer, 1997)
Vintage Fashions For Women: 1920s – 1940s (Schiffer, 1996)
Victorian & Edwardian Fashions For Women: 1840 – 1919 (Schiffer, 1995)
1914 Fashions (Ed., Dover, 1995)
59 Authentic Turn of the Century Fashion Patterns (Dover, 1994)

Bibliography/ Recommended Reading

Over the years, I have gleaned information from a variety of sources, including, but not limited to, professional lectures, historical documents and books, period magazines, theses and other scholarly papers, and books published for the public. Below, I have listed some of the most important reference books for information in this book; when it is a book that is generally available to the public at large, I have given brief information about it to help you determine whether it's something you, too, would like to read. Many books are in print and can be ordered through a local book dealer, but even out-of-print books can often be found; visit your local library and talk to the reference librarian about the inter-library loan.

Adams, Elizabeth D. *Aesthetic and Structural Restoration of an Early Twentieth Century Historic Costume.* Master's thesis, Colorado State University, 1980.

Arnold, Janet. *A Handbook of Costume.* S.G. Phillips, London, 1973.

Basic Principles for the Care and Preservation of Period Costumes. The National Museum of American History, Smithsonian Institution, Washington, D.C., undated.

Blum, Stella, ed. *Everyday Fashions of the Twenties.* Dover Publications, New York, 1981.
Pages of women's, children's, and men's fashions from Sears catalog.

___. *Everyday Fashions of the Thirties.* Dover Publications, New York, 1986.
Like the above book.

___. *Fashions & Costumes from Godey's Lady's Book.* Dover Publications, New York, 1985.
Reprints from the Victorian era's most famous fashion magazine, 1837 – 1869, including some color plates.

___. *Paris Fashions of the 1890s.* Dover Publications, New York, 1984.
Reprints of period fashion plates (some in color). These are exaggerated fashions, not what the average woman wore, but they give a good general guide to what was most fashionable in the 1890s.

___. *Ackerman's Costume Plates.* Dover Publications, New York, 1978.
Reprints of women's fashion pages from 1818 – 1828.

___. *Victorian Fashions & Costumes From Harper's Bazar.* Dover Publications, New York, 1974.
Reprints of high-fashion women's wear from 1867 – 1898.

Bradfield, Nancy. *Costume In Detail.* Plays Inc., New York, 1968.
This book is a must-have for those who collect women's fashions from 1730 to 1930. Consists of detailed drawings of both the outside and the inside of garments and includes information on fastenings, bustles, crinolines, and other construction details.

Collins, Maureen. *How To Wet-Clean Undyed Cotton And Linen.* Leaflet #478, Smithsonian Institution, Museum of History and Technology, Textile Laboratory, Washington, DC, 1967.

Cunnington, C. Willett. *English Women's Clothing in the Nineteenth Century.* Dover Publications, New York, 1990.
A detailed guide to women's fashions, 1800 – 1899, with line drawings. Though English fashions are chronicled here, these are generally the same styles Americans wore during this period.

___. *History of Underclothes, The.* Dover Publications, New York, 1992.
A study of Western underfashions for men and women from the Medieval Period through the 1920s.

Dalrymple, Priscilla Harris. *American Victorian Costume in Early Photographs.* Dover Publications, New York, 1991.
Authentic photographs of everyday American men, women, and children from the 1840s through the 1890s.

Directions For Constructing a Padded Hanger for Costumes and Guidelines for Hanging Costumes. Smithsonian Institution, Washington, D.C., undated.

Directions for Making Padded Hat Supports. Northampton Historical Society, undated.

Ewing, Elizabeth. *Dress & Undress.* B.T. Batsford, London, 1978.
A guide to women's underwear from ancient times through the 1970s.

Femmes fin de siécle. Musée de la Mode at du Costume, Paris, 1990.
Although the text is in French, even those who cannot read this language will benefit from the color photographs of exsisting women's garments from 1885 – 1895.

Finch, Karen, and Greta Putnam. *The Care and Preservation of Textiles.* B.T. Batsford, London, 1985.

Gernsheim, Alison. *Victorian & Edwardian Fashion: A Photographic Survey.* Dover Publications, New York, 1981.
Originally published in England under the title Fashion & Reality, *this book illustates women's, men's, and children's fashions from 1855 through the 1910s in period photographs (often of wealthy and fashionable people), along with excellent text on trends.*

Ginsburg, Madeleine, with Avril Hart, and Valerie D. Mendes. *Four Hundred Years of Fashion.* Victoria & Albert Museum, William Collins & Sons, New York, 1984.
This guide to women's and men's garments from c.1610 through the 1970s is primarily useful for its excellent color and black and white photos of authentic garments.

Goldberg, Michael Jay. *The Ties That Blind.* Schiffer Publishing, Atglen, PA, 1997. *Men's neckties from 1945 – 1975, with values.*

Harris, Kristina and Mare Yaroscak. *The Child in Fashion.* Schiffer Publishing, Atglen, PA, 1998.
A collector's guide to boys', girls', and babies' fashions, including values.

___. *59 Authentic Turn-of-the-Century Fashion Patterns.* Dover Publications, New York, 1994.
Period dressmaker's patterns (scaled) and detailed drawings of women's and some children's and men's fashions from 1890 – 1896.

___. *Victorian & Edwardian Fashions For Women: 1840 – 1919.* Schiffer Publishing, Atglen, PA, 1995.
A collector's guide with color photographs of authentic women's day and evening dresses, outerwear, underwear, and accessories with many historical ancedotes. Includes reform and fancy dress costumes and a value guide.

Bibliography/Recommended Reading

___. *Vintage Fashions For Women: 1920s – 1940s.* Schiffer Publishing, Atglen, PA, 1996.
Similar to the above book.

___. *Vintage Fashions For Women: the 1950s & 60s.* Schiffer Publishing, Atglen, PA, 1997.
Similar to the above book. Offers an unprecedented look at the ready-to-wear industry, including a list of popular ready-to-wear labels and designers.

Johnson, Judy M. *French Fashion Plates of the Romantic Era.* Dover Publications, New York, 1991.
Color reprints of women's fashion plates from 1830 – 1834; these are exaggerated versions of what the average woman actually wore.

LaBarre, Kathleen and Kay. *Reference Book of Children's Clothing: 1900 – 1919.* LaBarreBooks, Portland, OR, 1996.
An encyclopedic book covering garments and accessories with period illustrations.

___. *Reference Book of Men's Vintage Clothing: 1900 – 1919.* LaBarre Books, Portland, OR, 1993.
Like the above book.

___. *Women's Vintage Clothing: 1900 – 1919.* LaBarre Books, Portland, OR, 1992.
Like the above book.

___. *Reference Books of Women's Vintage Clothing: 1920 – 1929.* LaBarreBooks, Portland, OR, 1994.
Like the above book.

Langley, Susan. *Vintage Hats & Bonnets: 1770 – 1970.* Collector Books, Paducah, KY, 1998.

Lanker, Arlene Helen. *Historic Costume/Textile Collections in Small Museums: Management, Care, and Storage.* Master's thesis, Ohio State University, 1981.

Laubner, Ellie. *Fashions of the Roaring '20s.* Schiffer Publishing, Atglen, PA, 1996.
Primarily photographs of authentic women's and some men's and children's clothing and accessories of the 1920s, including values.

Lencek, Lena and Gideon Bosker. *Making Waves.* Chronicle Books, San Francisco, 1989.
Men's and women's swimwear from the turn of the century forward.

Museum of the City of New York. *American Lady & the Lady of London, The.* Dover Publications, New York, 1994.
Reprints of paper dolls from the 1850s – 1870s, showing typical styles of the era.

O'Hara, Georgina. *Encyclopedia of Fashion.* Harry N. Abrams, New York, 1986.
With notes on everything from designers to hat styles and bustle trends, this book compiles nineteenth and twentieth century fashion into an encyclopedic format. Emphasis is on c. 1900 forward.

Olian, JoAnne, ed. *Everyday Fashions: 1900 – 1920.* Dover Publications, New York, 1995.
Pages from Sears catalogs featuring fashions for women and children.

___. *Everyday Fashions of the Forties.* Dover Publications, New York, 1992.
Like the above book, but also featuring men's fashions.

___. *Children's Fashions.* Dover Publications, New York, 1994.
Reprints of drawings from a French fashion magazine featuring children's clothes from 1860 – 1912.

___. *Wedding Fashions.* Dover Publications, New York, 1994.
Reprints of drawings from a French fashion magazine illustrating bridal gowns and trousseaux.

Pest Busters. The Textile Museum, 1989.

Reilly, Maureen & Mary Beth Detrich. *Women's Hats of the 20th Century.* Schiffer Publishing, Atglen, PA, 1997.
   Over 600 color photos, plus good text on women's hats from the late Victorian era through the 1960s. Includes values.

Rose, Clare. *Children's Clothes.* B.T. Batsford, London, 1989.
   A history of children's and babies' wear from 1750 – 1985.

Sawin, Sylvia D. and the Boston Children's Museum. *Antique Fashion Paper Dolls of the 1890s.* Dover Publications, New York, 1984.
   Reprints of paper dolls from 1895 – 1896, showing fashionable costumes of the period.

Schoeffler, O.E. and William Dale. *Esquire's Encyclopedia of 20th Century Men's Fashion.* McGraw Hill, New York, 1973.

Smith, Charles H. Gibbs, ed. *The Fashionable Lady in the 19th Century.* Victoria & Albert Museum, London, 1960.
   Period drawings of women's garments from 1800 – 1900.

Smith, Desire. *Hats.* Schiffer Publishing, Atglen, PA, 1986.
   Color photographs of authentic period hats, primarily from the 1920s forward, but some dating as far back as 1800. Includes values.

Snyder, Jeffrey B. *Stetson Hats & the John B. Stetson Co. 1865 – 1970.* Schiffer Publishing, Atglen, PA, 1997.
   A thorough account of the Stetson company and its products along with values. The focus here is on men's hats, but women's hats are also covered.

Storing Old Garments in the Home. The Smithsonian Institution, Washington, D.C., undated.

Tarrant, Naomi. *Collecting Costumes.* George Allen & Unwin, London, 1983.

Thieme, Otto Charles, and Elizabeth Ann Coleman, Michelle Oberly, and Patricia Cunningham. *With Grace & Favour.* Cincinnati Art Museum, Cincinnati, 1993.
   Primarily color photographs of existing women's dresses from 1837 – 1912. Also text on reform and aesthetic costume.

Waugh, Nora. *Cut of Women's Clothes, The.* Routledge, New York, 1968.
   A guide to the cut and construction of period fashions 1600 – 1930, with scaled patterns.

___. *Cut of Men's Clothes, The.* Routledge, New York, 1968.
   Like the above book.

Willman, Paulette E. *Preservation of a Fan.* Master's thesis, Colorado State University, 1979.

Yonker, Crystal Ann. *An Investigation of Selected Cleaning Systems for the Preservation of 19th Century Cotton Fabric.* Master's thesis, Oklahoma State University, 1973.

Index